The Fabric of Myth

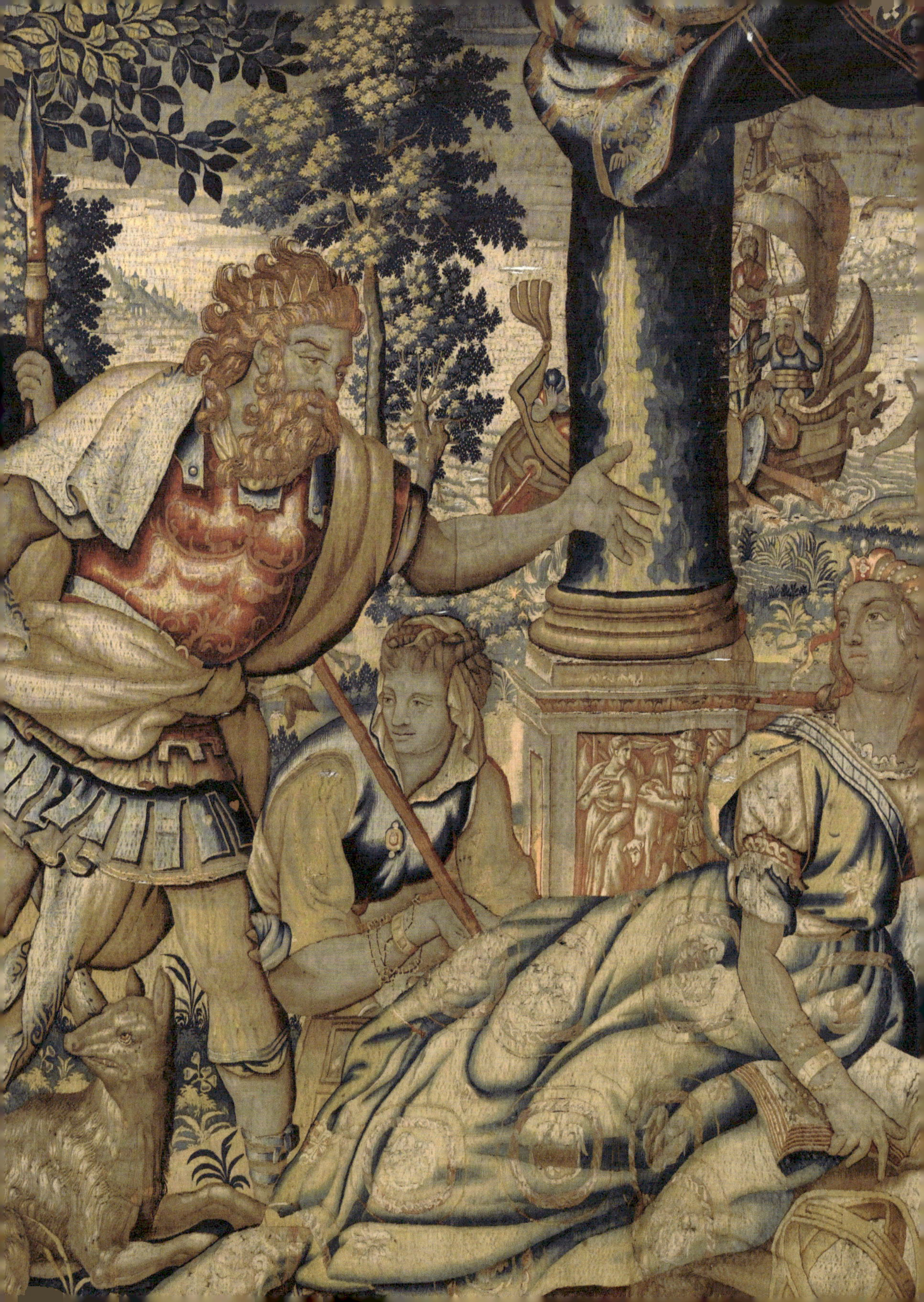

THE FABRIC OF MYTH

Compton Verney

Published by Compton Verney 2008

On the occasion of the exhibition
The Fabric of Myth
Compton Verney, 21 June – 7 September 2008

Curated by Antonia Harrison and James Young
Design Jaakko/o-sb.co.uk
Print Rosbeek, Netherlands

ISBN 978-0-9552719-4-6

supported by
PETER MOORES FOUNDATION

Compton Verney
Warwickshire CV35 9HZ
tel +44 (0) 1926 645500
www.comptonverney.org.uk
Registered charity No 1032478

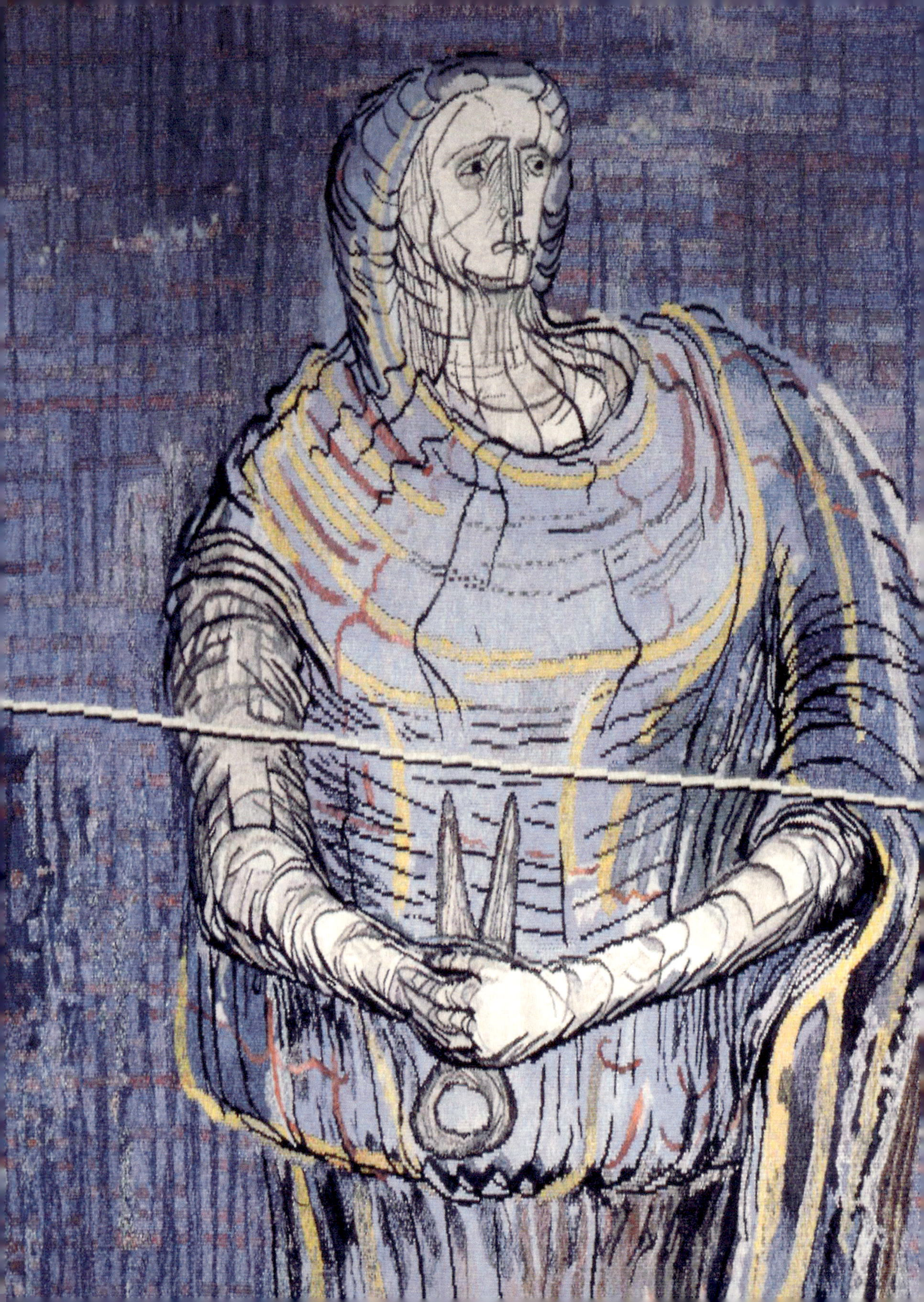

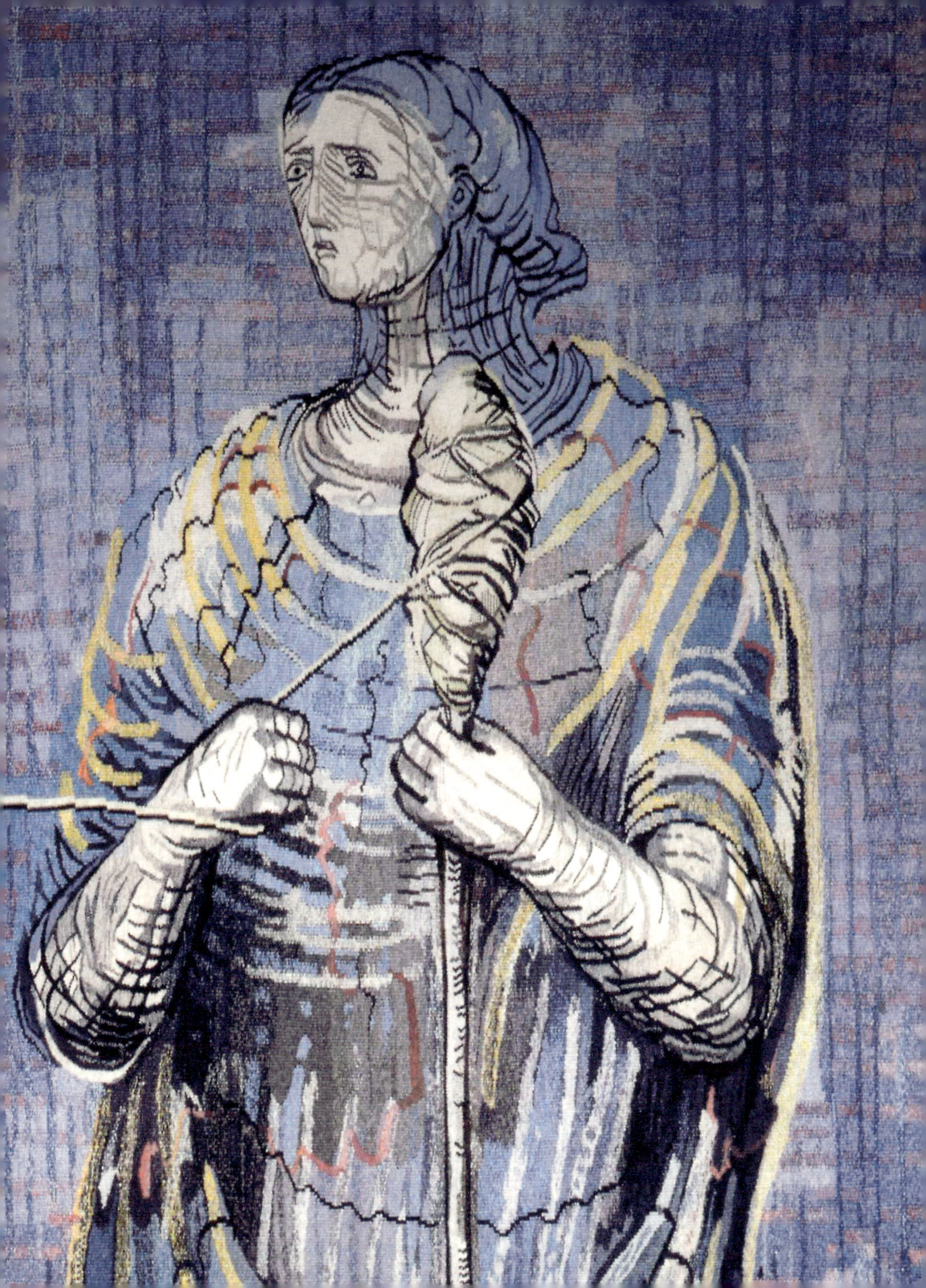

Foreword

Kathleen Soriano
Director, Compton Verney

The Fabric of Myth begins its journey in the world of textiles and classical myth. Ariadne's thread unlocked the mystery of the labyrinth; Penelope's loyalty to her husband Odysseus was tied to her loom as she wove and unwove by day and night; the Three Fates controlled the life span of both men and gods by spinning yarn, drawing out thread and cutting it. These narratives have stood the test of time.

In an age when textiles have become part of a throwaway culture, this exhibition uncovers the sometimes long-forgotten language of fabric and highlights the currency which the medium retains. The themes from these myths are explored in work from 400BC to the present day by artists as diverse as William Morris, Henry Moore, Bispo Do Rosário and Louise Bourgeois.

The Fabric of Myth continues to weave a symbolic path, and like the myths themselves, finds new relevance today. Testimony to this, are the responses to these themes by contemporary artists Shane Waltener and Delaine Le Bas. We are particularly grateful to them for engaging so imaginatively with the subject.

Thanks must also go to all the lenders and artists involved in this project. To Kathryn Sullivan Kruger for her insightful essay which forms the basis for the exploration of the myths in this catalogue, alongside the essays of co-curators Antonia Harrison and James Young. We are grateful once again to O-SB Design for their work on the catalogue and Rose-Innes Associates for their design of the exhibition graphics. We must also thank Raw Vision Magazine in particular for their early involvement and support with the exhibition. They have fostered long-standing relationships with a number of the lenders and artists in the show.

We should also like to thank Coats, Madeira Threads and PFAFF for their generous support of the learning and public programme associated with *The Fabric of Myth*. Recognition should also be given to the Exhibition Design Students at Buckinghamshire New University for embracing the opportunity to create an interactive space in response to the exhibition.

Finally, it goes without saying that such an exhibition would not be possible without the support of our Board of Governors and the team at Compton Verney.

Clues and Cloth: Seeking Ourselves in 'The Fabric of Myth'

Kathryn Sullivan Kruger

I dreamed there was an enormous web of beautiful fabric stretched out… covered all over with embroidered pictures. The pictures were illustrations of the myths of mankind but they were not just pictures, they were the myths themselves, so that the soft glittering web was alive.
–Doris Lessing, The Golden Notebook[1]

INTRODUCTION ~ THE WARP

The Sioux Indians tell a story about an ancient woman who lives alone in the wilderness weaving a blanket strip for her buffalo robe. A black dog curls at her feet. Nearby a kettle hangs over a fire, filled with a soup made of berries and roots. When the soup boils over, the dog barks to rouse the woman from her work. She hobbles over to the fire and stirs the soup, but as soon as she turns her back, the dog leaps up and unravels some of the threads. Eventually, the woman returns to her loom and resumes beating the design into the warp, row by row. Again, the soup boils over, and again the dog barks. The woman gets up, stirs her dinner, and as day follows night, weaving follows unravelling. Time moves slowly through the centuries while the old woman makes unhurried progress on her loom. It is said that when she completes her blanket, the world will come to an end.[2]

The supernatural world of weaving represented in this story exists in similar tales and myths in almost every culture throughout the world. For centuries weaving and cloth-making were vital forces that homogenised societies, both economically and imaginatively. Not only did weaving centres fuel great cities, but cloth performed the important function of reproducing a society's symbols, and, through these, its most significant principles and beliefs.

In *The Fabric of Myth*, the metaphoric dimensions of fabric are explored. With works ranging from a 4th century BC Boeotian drinking vessel to illuminated manuscripts, tapestry and embroideries both old and new, the exhibition brings together a collection that conveys a story about the capacity for fabric to speak across time. The exhibition's historical sweep offers a glimpse into the mysterious power of fabric, the notoriety and celebrity of its makers, the supernatural component of its production as well as its often fabled ability to confer authority and status, life and death.

A piece of fabric transmits information about the society which created it in a manner not dissimilar to a written language, except in this case the grammar is printed in the cloth's fibre, pattern, dye, and method of production. For centuries this technology supported empires. It is said that during the reign of Elizabeth I, a candidate for knighthood knelt on a sack of wool as a potent reminder that the country's power relied on its weaving industry. Likewise, weaving has long been a metaphor for the creation of something other than cloth – a story, a plot, or a world. Its production represents society's earliest textual practices. Whether a beaded collar, a woven blanket, or an embroidered sampler, each of these tells a story significant to the time in which it was created. When gathered together, these artefacts embody a universal narrative of humanity's sacred and secular practices and beliefs.

The weaver or cloth-maker has often represented the qualities of a Creator figure. Just as a cloth can be woven and a world created, so can it be unravelled and destroyed. Virtually all ancient civilizations attributed the craft of weaving to a god or goddess. Among the most famous are Isis of Egypt (who invented weaving with the help of her sister, Nephthys), Ixchel of the Mayans, Tlazolteotle of Mexico, Spider Woman of the

Navajo (Diné), Mokusa of Russia, Uttu from ancient Sumer, Toci of pre-Columbian Mexico, Athena of Greece, Ukemochi of Japan, and Brahma / Maya of India. Consequently, any human beings who wove were often considered to possess supernatural powers.

In English many words exist that connect cloth-making with storytelling, testifying to centuries of our experience at the loom. Like a piece of fabric, a written or spoken story may be spun, woven, knitted, quilted, sewn, or pieced together. We talk about the 'fabric' of our society when characterising our collective ideas. Our thoughts and emotions can 'unravel', 'tangle', or 'fray'. Sometimes our ideas have too many 'loose ends', a term that originally meant something woven but not yet tied off the loom and in danger of falling apart. When we describe work or thoughts as 'shoddy', we are using a word that once referred to poorly woven material sold at greatly reduced prices. Someone dreamy or inattentive is said to be 'woolgathering', which alludes to the actual profession of a woolgatherer who appeared to wander aimlessly through the fields, gathering tufts of wool from the branches and bushes that flocks rubbed against while grazing. Although attesting to the importance of cloth-making in human history, these terms no longer have any explicit reference to cloth but are now used almost exclusively to describe the realm of human emotions and mental activity.

WEAVING THE PLOT

Now it appears to me that almost any Man may, like the Spider, spin from his own inward his own airy Citadel... full of Symbols for his spiritual eye, of softness for his spiritual touch, of space for his wandering.
–John Keats in a letter to J.H. Reynolds[3]

Weaving dates back to the Paleolithic period; one of the oldest known woven fragments was identified in 1995 from pieces of clay impressed with the pattern of a textile or basket, dating from between 24,870 and 26,980 years ago.[4] Language, too, is steeped in our experience of cloth-making. In English the verb *to weave* indicates not just the making of textiles but any creative act. The noun *text* comes from the Latin verb *texere*,

Fig. 1 *Ariadne (detail)* [2]

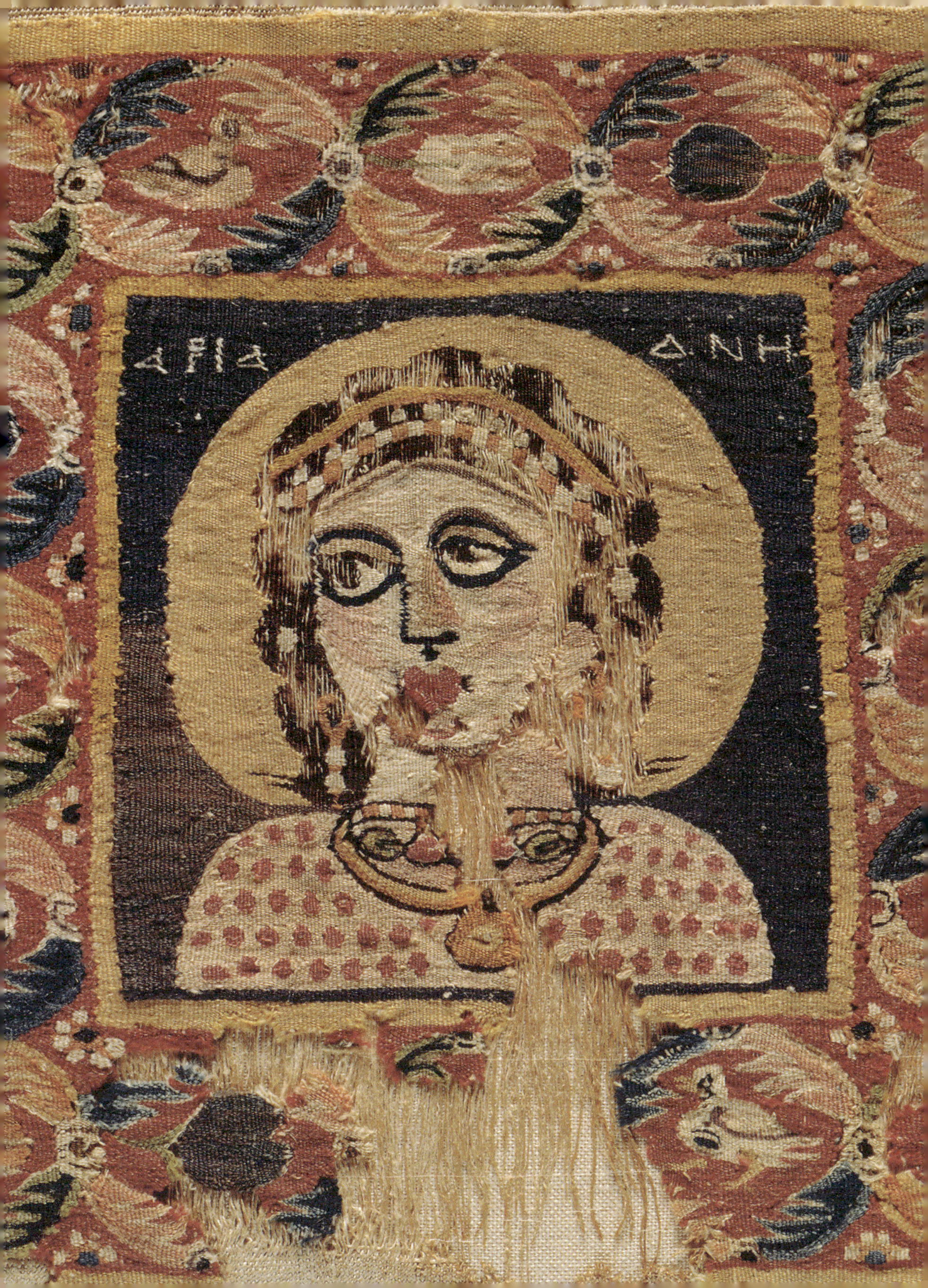
ΑΓΙΑ ΑΝΗ

also meaning 'to construct or to weave'. In Greek the noun *tekhne* refers to art, craft, and skill, and in Arabic the word *tiraz* (sometimes *taraz*) is used to describe both weaving cloth and composing poems. In many languages a weaver not only fashions textiles but can, with the same verb, contrive texts.

In cloth-making or storytelling, one begins with a thread. One thread, one thought. The legendary figure of the storyteller belongs to Ariadne, the jilted lover of Theseus who went on to marry the god Dionysus. When Theseus faced his battle with the Minotaur, it was Ariadne who gave him clever counsel, giving him a ball of thread to wind his way through the labyrinth and find his way back, for even if Theseus were able to kill the man-bull, he would certainly become caught in the labyrinth's web.

Ariadne's thread represents a story's narrative, for it is the storyteller who creates a labyrinth of thought, leading her listener into another world where the narrative unfolds and eventually returning her audience to the world of light and possibility, forever transformed by the tale. Throughout time the plot of Ariadne's thread has been re-told in different ways, but each deals with the same problem: protagonists (and their audiences) are offered clues to find their way out of a forest, a poem, a story, or a maze. No accident that the word *clue* originally derives from the Anglo-Saxon *cliwen*, meaning 'ball of yarn'. In this exhibition we, too, are offered clues with an invitation to trace our way through history's labyrinth and consider the ways that cloth has wielded such extraordinary power in shaping the world around us.

Complementing the important figure of Ariadne as cloth-maker and storyteller, a woollen tapestry from Egypt [fig. 1], 5th century AD forms a pair with Dionysus (not shown). The youngest god in the Greek pantheon, Dionysus finds Ariadne after her abandonment by Theseus, weds her and restores her status. In the ancient world Ariadne was appealed to by worshippers for protection and liberation. In this remarkable piece, Ariadne gazes left, presumably at the companion textile of Dionysus. Her eyes, seductively outlined with kohl, portray her as an Egyptian-looking goddess, complete with a mandorla (halo). The talismanic border both frames her and suggests the divinity of her nature.

All weavers or cloth-makers, however, were not benign. The sorceress and weaver, Circe, depicted on a Boeotian drinking vessel [fig. 2] can be seen weaving cloth as well as stirring a potion for a terrified Odysseus. To the right of Circe

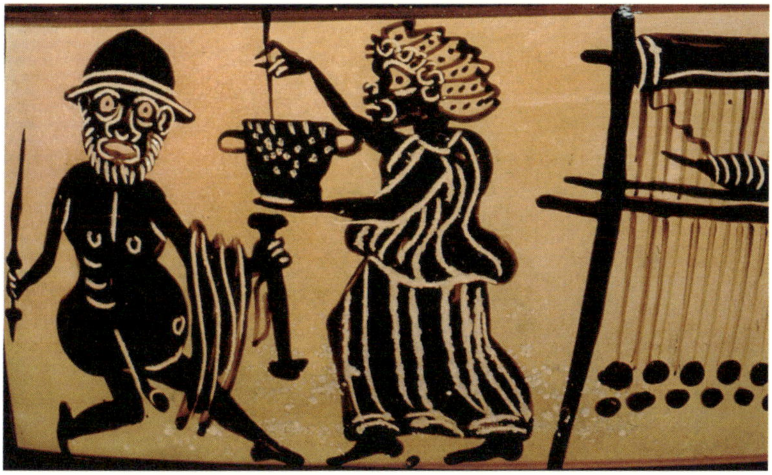

Fig. 2 *Odysseus and Circe (detail)* [5]

stands her loom. Like all women in Ancient Greece, whether queens or slaves, Circe is a weaver. In this representation she is turned away from her weaving, yet its presence connotes the mythic and magical dimensions that weaving implied in the ancient world. What we know about the craft during this age derives from archaeological remains as well as from friezes, wall paintings and, as in this case, vase painting, all of which record the style of looms and the way wool was carded and spun. Pottery from this period shows warp-weighted looms built according to the dimensions of the desired textile. Clay weights steadied the warp strings so that one or two weavers could pass a shuttle through the warp threads with the cloth woven from the top to the bottom of the loom.[5] In this depiction we see Circe's cloth rolled tidily at the top with her shuttle tucked between the threads. Clearly she is in the midst of weaving, just as she is in the midst of hatching a plot to ensnare Odysseus. The painting refers to a scene in Homer's *The Odyssey* when Circe, having already turned his men into swine, plans the same fate for Odysseus. Unknown to her, however, Odysseus has already eaten the antidote to her poison given to him by Hermes.

Literature from Ancient Greece often illustrates how a woven object embodies the psychology of its weaver and how weaving can become a metaphor for the weaver's thought processes. Scenes abound wherein women like Helen of Troy, Clytemnestra and Penelope are depicted weaving plots as well as garments. The Greek language links together these two different activities so that "woven fabric, poetry, and *mētis* [craftiness] are all delineated with the verb 'to sew' or 'to weave'".[6] When Homer depicts nymphs such as Circe and Calypso, he often introduces them into a narrative which depicts them simultaneously singing and weaving. When Odysseus' men (and later, Odysseus) first glimpse Circe, Homer writes:

> *They stood there in the forecourt of the goddess with the glorious hair, and heard Circe inside singing in a sweet voice as she went up and down a great design on a loom, immortal such as goddesses have, delicate and lovely and glorious their work.*
> *–Homer, The Odyssey* X[7]

This linguistic dimension to cloth-making suggests the weaver's ability to conjure subtle webs, plots and spells. Scenes of deception were very popular in Greek literature. Whether concerning the gift of a Trojan horse, a plot to deceive a Cyclops, or a winding thread to escape a labyrinth, stories from Greek mythology and poetry satisfy because their protagonists – human or divine – know how to shape plots craftily. This quality of *mētis*, as it was known, can today best be understood as the idea of cunning. Like mētis, cunning means more than deception. Born of wit, it is the trait most esteemed by the Ancient Greeks, perhaps because it was the trait that kept heroes, like Odysseus, alive even when circumstances were against them.

Originally Mētis was the daughter of the father of all the Gods, Oceanus. The ancients called her 'patron of good counsel' because she had access to more knowledge than any other god before or after her birth. After the Titans were ousted, Mētis remained with the Olympians because she had helped them defeat Cronos (Zeus' father). Beautiful and clever, Mētis was a shape-changer. Eventually, Zeus impregnated her. After a series of events which proved hazardous for Mētis, Zeus swallowed her, and he, instead, gave birth to their child, Athena, who exploded from his head fully armed for battle. Although dedicated to serving her father, Athena exhibits many of her mother's qualities. Like Mētis, Athena is a shape-changer and is known for her wisdom and cunning. She was also worshipped by the Athenians as the inventor of the loom and therefore forms a direct link to the idea of mētis and weaving.

Athena, however, was not the only deity in Olympus with a talent for weaving and deception. Homer tells us that when Odysseus was stranded on the island of the Phaiakians, he listens to a song about the adulterous affair between Ares and Aphrodite, the god of war and the goddess of love. Hephaestus, Aphrodite's husband and smithy to the gods, becomes incensed; in retaliation, he weaves a plot that takes the shape of a web in which to ensnare his wife and her lover:

> *Now when, in his anger against Ares, he had made this treacherous snare, he went to his chamber where his own dear bed lay,*
> *and spun his fastenings around the posts from every direction, while many more were suspended overhead, from the roof beams, thin,*
> *like spider webs, which not even one of the blessed gods could see.*
> *He had fashioned it to be very deceptive.*
> –*Homer, The Odyssey* VIII

When Ares and Aphrodite are caught *in flagrante delicto*, Hephaestus invites the rest of the Olympians into his chamber to laugh at the couple ensnared in his mētis.

The most famous of weaving stories, however, belongs to Penelope. The stylised engraving by John Flaxman [31] illustrates her tale, which has captured the imagination of people throughout the Western world for centuries. Her latest rediscovery came in Victorian England. Understandably, Penelope's focused dedication to her husband and son became a powerful standard for the middle-class Victorian wife. According to Homer's story, a band of young, hot-blooded suitors move into the estate belonging to Odysseus and Penelope while Odysseus is away on his homeward voyage. The suitors abuse the privileges given to guests by dining excessively off their hosts' food and wine, sleeping with their servants and refusing to leave. To protect herself, Penelope maintains a separate life from the suitors, and every appearance she makes is done on her own terms. In this way she maintains an illusion of autonomy when in reality she is no more free than a slave.

In Ancient Greece the women's chambers were built at the back of the house (or, in Penelope's case, on the second floor). Called the *gynaikonitides*, these quarters were especially designed to guard the women, as well as to confine them. If a woman wanted to leave the gynaikonitides, she would have to obtain permission from those in the men's 'public' quarters. In Penelope's case, she would have to pass through the suitors' territory and risk unwanted physical contact with them. Because she is unable to move freely about her home, Penelope remains isolated and in a state of siege. Her body, metaphorically, represents the last room in the palace that must be won, since access to Penelope would guarantee the throne. In her desperate hope that Odysseus will return, Penelope placates the suitors by telling them that she will choose a new husband once she has completed the weaving of a shroud for her ailing father-in-law as her final duty to Odysseus' family (an obligation that was expected from a family's eldest daughter).

Weaving was compulsory in Ancient Greece and it was most often accomplished in the secure and secured gynaikonitides. Immured in the private sphere, women contributed to the public sphere by producing textiles not only for home use but for gifts, religious offerings and commercial trade.[8] Every estate was expected to have a reserve of cloth; difference in the quality indicated social status and extent of wealth. The gynaikonitides, where men rarely had access, became in Penelope's story a realm of subtlety and stratagem, the place where she discovered and fulfilled her plan to escape the suitors and the male authority which they represented.

Although Homer never describes the pattern on Laertes' shroud, Penelope must have been weaving a storytelling cloth. A simple winding cloth could have been completed in a matter of weeks and would not have been complex enough to deceive the suitors for almost four years. Every day she weaves an intricate pattern complementing the high station of her father-in-law and every night, once her servants and suitors have fallen asleep, she picks out the pattern and unravels most of the threads she has woven that day. Since the intricacies of cloth-making did not concern men in this society, they were easily duped. Who knows how long her trick would have lasted if one of Penelope's servants had not betrayed her. Seduced by one of the suitors, the servant gives away the secret that all of the women must have known.

Although Penelope cannot change the circumstances of her life, nor alter the course of her husband's return, she opens a space of possibility by delaying a fate that seems unavoidable. During the day she makes steady progress towards this destiny, but at night she unravels the advances she has made. Just as a chess piece moves back and forth between two positions in an effort to delay the inevitable checkmate, so Penelope weaves and unweaves her cloth in an effort to create a pause or break in the momentum that is propelling her towards a future that she is desperate to avoid.

In this exhibition an embroidered picture shows a pensive Penelope holding Odysseus' bow on her lap [30]. Rather than grasping a shuttle – the instrument with which she deceived the suitors who tried to pressure her into re-marriage – she clutches an instrument of war which will in due course provide the means by which the suitors are driven from her home. Likewise, in Penelope's hands, the shuttle becomes a tool for combat. However, this battle is waged not in the open field but in private quarters. Penelope's story therefore emphasises the socio-sexual politics of Ancient Greece, and also establishes a setting for other legendary weavers.

The story of Arachne, re-told by the 8th century Roman poet, Ovid, further testifies to the ability of weaving to convey meaning and wield power. The late 15th century Holkham Hall manuscript [fig. 3] offers an intriguing example of how ancient myths were appropriated by the dominant culture of the day (in this case 15th century Catholic England) and re-told to sanction that power, occasionally with minor alterations. In just four scenes this manuscript portrays the essential elements of the Athena and Arachne myth as recorded in Book VI of the *Metamorphoses*.

According to Ovid's tale, Arachne is a young woman without title or birthright, but with great renown for her weaving. Unwisely, she brags that her work is without equal. Her skill, according to Ovid, was so great that:

The nymphs would leave their vineyards of Tmolus,
And rise out of the waters of Pactolus,
Not merely to admire work that's done,
But to enjoy the sight of making it...
–*Ovid, Metamorphoses* VI

Affronted by the young woman's pride, Athena (believed by the Athenians to have invented weaving) appears in the guise of an old woman and offers Arachne a chance to repent and at the same time placate the gods (in this case, Athena herself). When Arachne remains impenitent, Athena challenges her to a weaving contest, at the conclusion of which Athena, angered by Arachne's obstinacy and skill, strikes her so hard with a shuttle that the ashamed Arachne hangs herself. Athena, in pity we are told by Ovid, turns the young girl into a spider, an arachnid:

to swing, to live now and forever,
even to the last hanging creature of your kind.
–*Ovid, Metamorphoses* V[9]

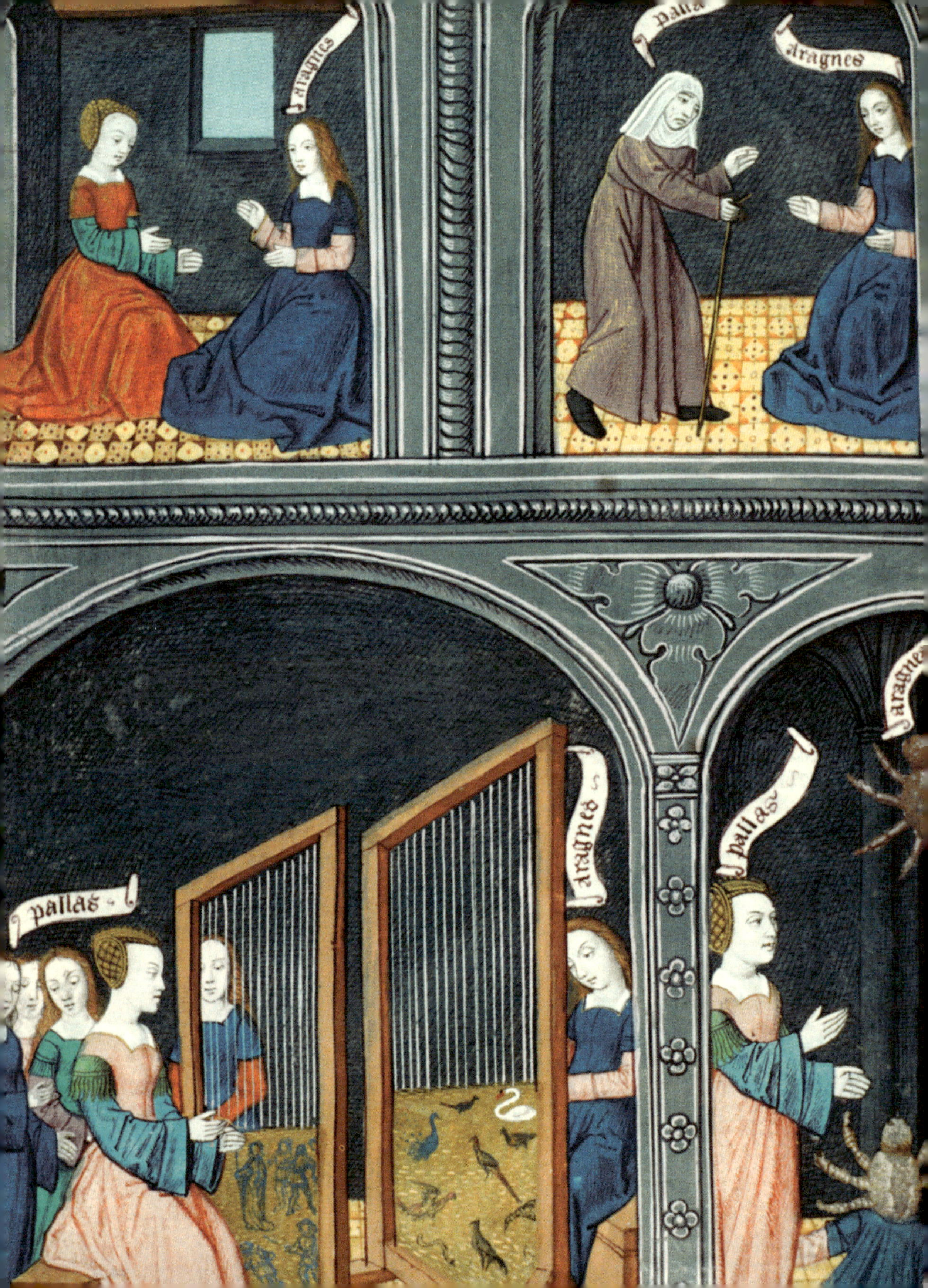
aragnes
aragnes
pallas
aragnes
pallas
aragnes

In Ancient Greece, death by hanging was reserved for thieves and criminals. Ovid leaves little doubt that Arachne loses the contest for power, but the poet lets the reader decide whether or not she loses the contest for skill. In his version of the myth, Athena weaves scenes of war, fate, the inexorable will of the gods and, as a warning to Arachne, the punishments doled out to mortals who have previously challenged the gods' authority; conversely, Arachne weaves the crimes of the gods, their misuse of power and their victimization of mortal women. This subtext occurs throughout Ovid's story even though it does not constitute its principal theme. Readers throughout the centuries have generally glossed over these nuances so that the story of Athena and Arachne has usually been viewed as a warning to those women or men who challenge any sanctioned political system. The Holkham Hall manuscript subscribes to such a view, but the illuminator provides interesting details not found in the original source.

In the first panel of the manuscript Arachne sits beside a noblewoman above whose head appears the name *Pallas*. Pallas is another name for Athena and one of the word's Greek meanings, 'a brandisher of a spear' gives the epithet an authority which, in this telling, places the noblewoman in a position of strength. Arachne's hair is long and untied, indicating that she is young and, perhaps, unrestrained, whereas the noblewoman's hair is concealed and crowned in a beaded cap. In the first frame, Arachne appears to be bragging to the noblewoman about her skill. In the next frame, Pallas appears as an aged nun, exhorting Arachne to repent. The nun's disguise sets up intriguing questions. Bearing in mind that the noblewoman/nun wields both earthly and spiritual power, the third panel in which the weaving contest is illustrated depicts Pallas weaving human shapes – the domain of worldly and spiritual authority – whereas by contrast Arachne's loom is woven with birds, a visual allusion to the metamorphosis which greets us in the fourth and final panel in which Pallas transforms Arachne's head into a giant spider.

Literature from Ancient Greece tells us that Athena's nemesis was the spider, a creature most despised by her. Although unsavoury to this Greek goddess, spider figures were not always considered vile in the ancient world. For

Fig. 3 *Arachne and Athena weaving contest (detail)* [11]

many African tribes and for almost all of the Indian tribes of the North American Plains, the spider as weaver is considered a beneficent creature, a creator and a trickster. Anansi the Spider occupies many African folk tales; indeed, his primary function is to weave stories, generally about his own escapades. Relying on his innate qualities of cunning and 'art-ifice,' Anansi tells us that he once captured leopard, python, hornet and Mmoatia the fairy and sold them to the Sky God in exchange for the Sky God's stories. In a historically derived contemporary clothing fabric produced in the UK for the African textile market [13], a spider sits within the centre of stars and moons. If this fabric's pattern represents the cosmos, then Anansi is its creator.

A striking anecdote that associates language with spiders and their webs occurs in speculations that the alphabet was discovered by tracing the mysterious angles of a spider's web. Conjectural as this statement might sound, it intrigues nevertheless. Given the fact that our early ancestors studied the natural world so closely, finding it full of mysteries that still elude us today, it is conceivable (albeit unknowable) that the spider's web suggested an early form of an alphabet.[10] In the spider figure we confront a being who represents thought and whose web constitutes the material produced from thought. Similar to a web, thought is spun from the body of a thinking, creating being. This metaphor implies that whether we spin fibres or thoughts, human beings participate in a system that clothes society in the fabric of belief as well as the fabric of cloth.

MESSAGES IN CAPTIVITY

And what shall Philomela do? A guard prevents her flight; stout walls of solid stone fence in the hut; speechless lips can give no token of her wrongs. But grief has sharp wits, and in trouble cunning comes. She hangs a Thracian web on her loom, and skillfully weaving purple signs on a white background, she thus tells the story of her wrongs.
–Ovid, Metamorphoses VI

The artist Elaine Reichek's embroidered sampler entitled *Ovid's Weavers* [fig. 4], offers an alternative reading of the Arachne myth alongside its sister story 'Tereus, Procne, and Philomela' (also from Book VI of the *Metamorphoses*). Here, Reichek highlights the subversive and highly suggestive elements in both tales by stitching two quatrains from each story side-by-side:

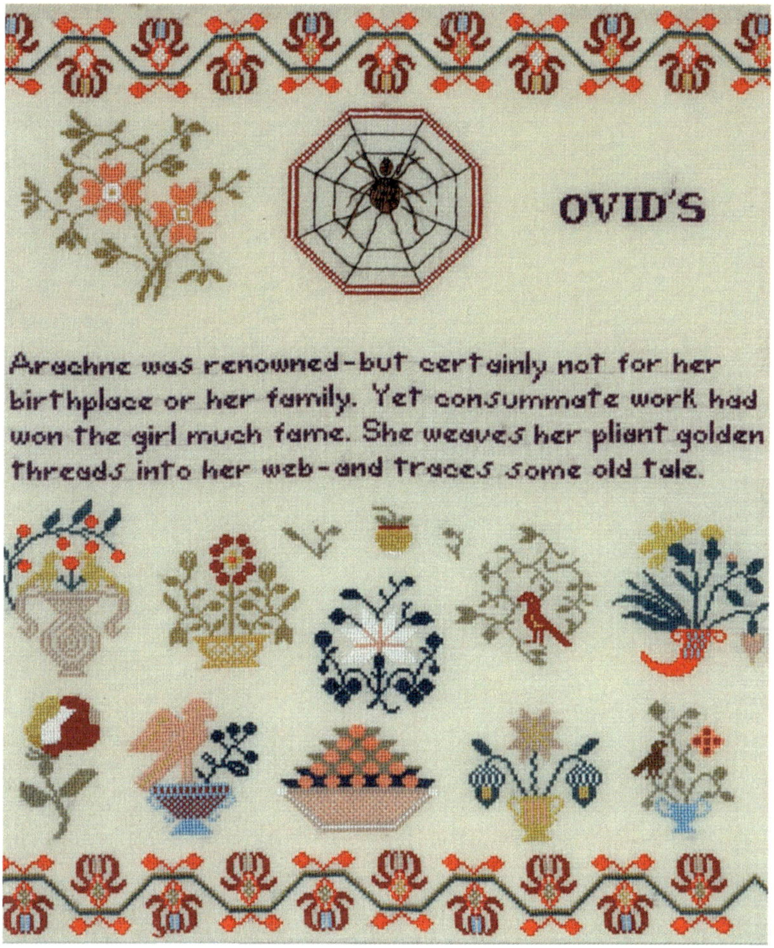

Fig .4 Elaine Reichek *Sampler (Ovid's Weavers) (detail)* [12]

Arachne's emphasise her skill, whereas Philomela's underscore her determination to articulate injustice.

The Philomela/Procne myth is the more violent of the two stories. In Ovid's account, the Athenian princess, Procne, is married to a Theban man, a foreigner, named Tereus. He takes her to Thebes, which was considered by the Athenians to be a barbaric country. After a year Procne grows lonely and requests her husband to return to Athens to fetch her sister, Philomela. On the return journey, he rapes Philomela and holds her captive in a hut. When she threatens to reveal his terrible crime, Tereus cuts out her tongue, returns to Thebes and tells his wife that Philomela died on their passage home. Meanwhile, a desperate Philomela weaves a tapestry wherein she describes what has happened to her and where she can be found. Procne, who receives the tapestry and deduces its meaning, rescues her sister. Together they plan a savage revenge, murdering Tereus and Procne's own children. As punishment for their crimes, Procne, Philomela and Tereus are turned into birds by the gods. The lines from Ovid that Reichek selects for her embroidery, however, constitute the story's turning point, a hiatus between two acts of violence, when Philomela defiantly tells her story through the voice of her loom.[11]

To a large extent Reichek's sampler effaces the violence of this story; her needlepoint shows pretty flowers and skilful stitches which sweetly demonstrate her skill. Furthermore, her choice of media is intriguing. In the 18th and 19th centuries, samplers were generally embroidered by young women prior to marriage, showing their proficiency at needlework and in many cases suggesting they were ready to wed. Paradoxically, Reichek insinuates a different message altogether: she turns this seemingly innocuous medium on its head by embroidering four lines from Ovid's story which warn her 'reader' that she will neither be diminished nor controlled, but will instead, "on a white background, weave[s] purple / signs: the letters that denounce the savage crime." What this crime refers to – Philomela's plight or the artist's – cannot be known, but Reichek's intent is clear. She will not be silenced, but will use all her skill to "invent, in/misery."

When approached from Reichek's perspective, Ovid's two myths emerge as accounts of women who, relying on their own mētis, operate outside established authority. Above each quatrain, Reichek embroiders their symbols, a spider above Arachne's lines and a bird above Philomela's. What these mean – freedom, skill, or danger – the reader must choose. In the hands of Reichek, the sampler has metamorphosed into a written declaration of caution and personal power.

Another mythic weaver, derived from these Greek prototypes, *The Lady of Shalott*, has fascinated artists and readers alike since the 19th century when Lord Alfred Tennyson published his poem of that name (c. 1832–1848). At least seven different Pre-Raphaelite artists illustrated her – Dante Gabriel Rossetti, Elizabeth Siddal, John Millais, Sidney Meteyard, John William Waterhouse, Edward Burne-Jones, and William Holman Hunt. The engraving by William Holman Hunt is one of the most famous of these [fig. 5]. According to Tennyson's poem, *The Lady of Shalott* begins as a lighthearted, romantic tale that two-thirds of the way through the poem turns into a story of inexplicable longing and unavoidable death.

In the first section of the four-part poem, Tennyson describes a castle built on a small island, surrounded by lilies and connected to Camelot by a road which winds along the mainland shore and by the traffic of boats that sail past the island. Although the castle is plainly seen, no one has ever glimpsed its inhabitant, but the farmers occasionally hear a woman singing. In the second section the poet moves away from the external landscape and focuses on the tower's interior. Here, the Lady is described as weaving a wonderful web, working into its design scenes from Camelot which are shown to her through a magic mirror. The reader is then told that she must look at Camelot only through the mediation of the mirror. If, instead, she gazes directly out of the window towards Camelot, she will be cursed.

In the third section Tennyson introduces Lancelot, who moves first in the landscape outside the tower and then 'flashes' into the private, enclosed space of the tower through the Lady's mirror. Simultaneous with his entry into her room via this mirror, the Lady hears him singing outside her window. Leaving her loom, she walks over to the window to gaze down upon him and thus releases the curse: the mirror cracks and her tapestry unravels. In the fourth section of the poem, the Lady moves irrevocably towards death.

In the figure of the Lady of Shalott we can read a composite of all the weavers we encounter in this exhibition: not only does she derive from Greek (and Teutonic) mythology – particularly its link between weaving, sorcery and fate – but she is also a spider figure, like Anansi, a storyteller who ultimately finds herself caught in her own web. Hunt's engraving illustrates the moment when the curse is released and the weaver is caught in its fury as the fabric on the loom unravels. Standing inside the frame of her loom where the cloth is woven, she becomes implicated in the story she is creating rather than remaining outside her own work. As she tries to disentangle the threads from the lower half of her body, we sense immediately that a transformation is about to take place: just as it did for Arachne, the weaver becomes entangled in her own story, subjected to the power of her own art which she is unable to control. In the poem, the Lady of Shalott at first seems an independent authority like one of the Fates of Ancient Greece, but as the poem progresses and as Hunt strongly suggests, she becomes merely another victim who cannot escape her own destiny.

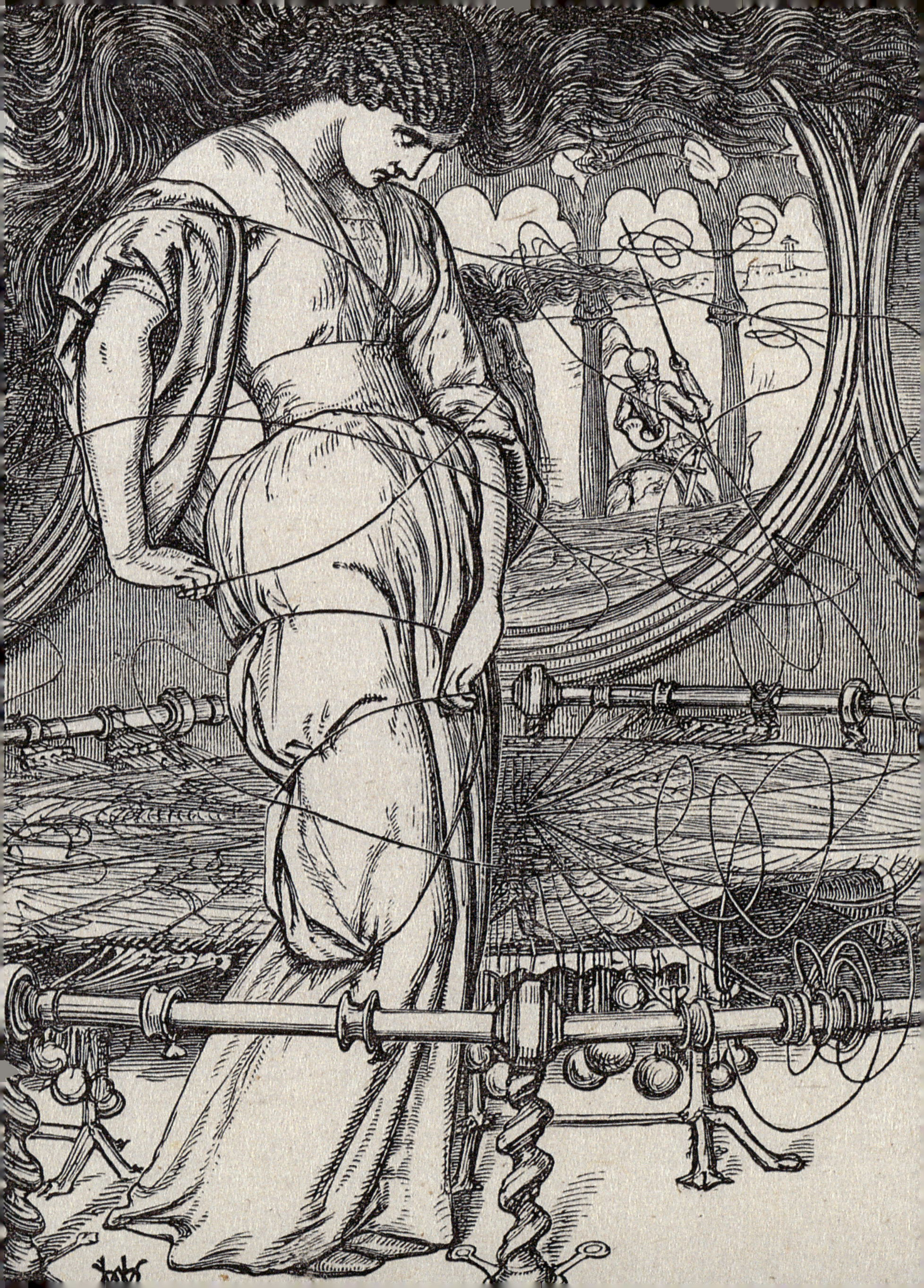

The relationship between cloth-making and imprisonment was not merely a subject of myth or literature however, but one of history. For hundreds, perhaps thousands of years, people imprisoned often turned to cloth-making as a means of occupying themselves through the long hours of each day. In the Yuma Territorial Prison of Arizona, male inmates from the late 19th – early 20th centuries were taught the tedious yet delicate craft of lace-making. The incentive of creating lace was part of a reward system which promised to reduce prison sentences in turn for the 'good behaviour' offered through handiwork. The Yuma Prison exemplifies one of many cloth-making industries that existed in the United States and in colonial Europe for over three centuries.

Handiwork accomplished during imprisonment was executed by all members of society, from slaves to queens. This exhibition contains three embroideries by Mary Queen of Scots [17] made during her nineteen-year imprisonment in England (1568–87). Their existence illuminates the often deeper connection between cloth and its maker, between the object and its creation. Mary's communicative powers were limited and controlled during her incarceration and needlework became more than a pastime to her. In her embroidery and its symbolism she found a way to convey the injustice of her situation.

Juxtaposed against the Queen's artistry is the work of Ray Materson, who taught himself embroidery while in prison. Much of his work illuminates the psychology of captivity. In *First Cigarette* and *Don't Get Pulled In* [19, 20], the artist depicts the terror of addiction. In both cases, the victim is surrounded by forces he's incapable of controlling. In another embroidery, *Tiny, Life×6, The Noon Watch* [21], the artist portrays a man inside a prison; however, because he stands outside the interior space of the bedroom which is barred even through the opened door, the artist suggests a movement towards freedom. *Metamorphosis III* [23] completes the artist's psychological journey from captivity to freedom; although still imprisoned by a cocoon, the butterfly looks ready to emerge and follow the others which flutter in the distance.

In works such as these we are confronted with the mental landscape of artists whose personal stories imbue the cloth they make with significance. Whether an engraving of the mythical

Fig. 5 William Holman Hunt *The Lady of Shalott (detail)* [9]

Lady of Shalott, the tapestries from a 16th century queen, or the needlework of modern artists like Reichek and Materson, these works are significant both because of the context of their making and the hand of their maker.

DESTINY & MEMORY

...but there in the future he shall endure all that his destiny and the heavy Spinners spun for him with the thread at his birth...
–*The Odyssey* VII

Greek mythology links weaving to fate, and cloth-making to the notion of creating a personal destiny. Not surprisingly, Greek culture exhibited an ambiguous attitude towards cloth-making and cloth-makers, one most probably rooted in its projection of 'Fate', which was represented by three mythic figures called the Moirai. Even Zeus, the chief of all gods, had to submit to their will.

In Henry Moore's tapestry of the Fates [15], we encounter the Moirai: Klotho, the maiden, spins the thread of life; Lachesis, the matron, allots its length; and Atropos, the crone, cuts the life-thread. The youngest, Klotho, stands on the tapestry's right, her robes swirling around her narrow figure as if she, too, were a distaff filled with an expanse of potentiality. The middle-aged Lachesis frames the left portion of the canvas; her figure is full, suggestive of pregnancy. Atropos, whose name means 'inexorable' or 'inevitable', stands between her younger sisters, looking more haggard; the yellow lines Moore traces in her figure suggest the shape of an hourglass. The significance is clear: at any moment her scissors, poised to sever the thread of life, could make their final cut. What arrests the viewer is the intense look of sorrow on all three faces. The life of someone literally stretches between their hands, but rather than exchanging looks of maniacal control or indifference, the sisters gaze at each other with expressions of grief. Klotho seems to be tightening the thread in preparation for Atropos who is about to cut in the middle of its length, shortening the life of whomever the thread represents. Moore keeps to the Ancient Greek tradition of depicting the Fates as three sisters who together represent three stages of life, although he departs from a convention which often feared

Fig. 6 Tilleke Schwarz *Losing our Memory (detail)* [38]

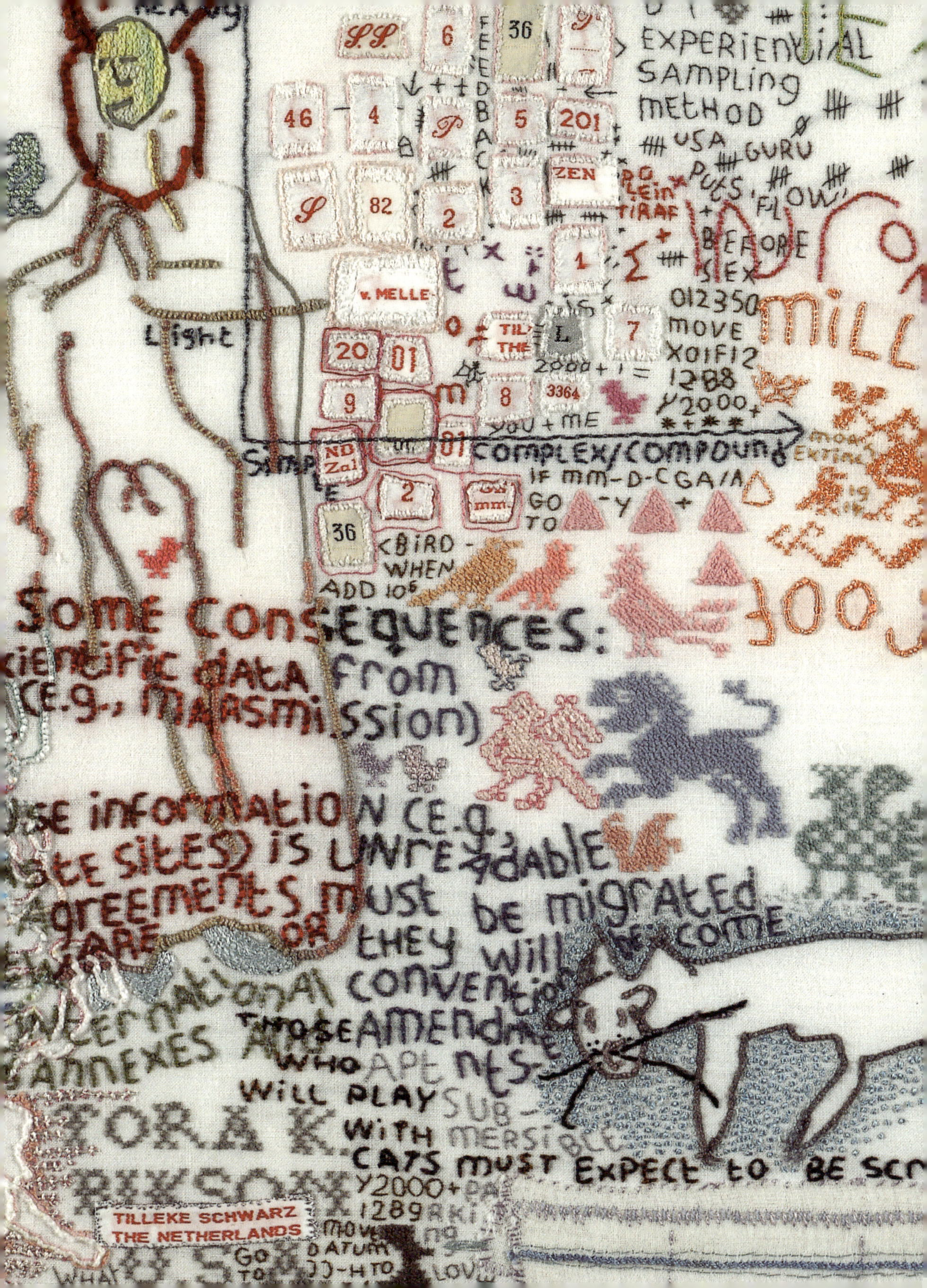

EXPERIENTIAL
SAMPLING
METHOD
USA GURU
PUTS 'FLOW'
BEFORE
SEX
012350
MOVE
X01F12
1288
Y2000+
2000+1=
YOU+ME
COMPLEX/COMPOUND
IF MM-D-CGA/A
GO
TO
BIRD-
WHEN
ADD 10⁶
Light
v. MELLE
ZEN
SOME CONSEQUENCES:
from
ssion)
information (e.g.
is unreadable
agreements must be migrated
they will become
conventions
amendments
annexes
THOSE
WHO ARE
WILL PLAY
WITH
CATS MUST EXPECT TO BE SCR
TILLEKE SCHWARZ
THE NETHERLANDS
Y2000+
1289
MOVE
DATUM
GO
TO

and vilified the sisters by rendering them as sympathetic and reluctant arbiters of life and death.[12]

Just as fabric can be seen as a metaphor for a future destiny, it can also take the shape of a life lived and form a potent retainer of memory. In Euripides' play *Ion*, the mother Kreusa who is impregnated by Apollo abandons her newborn child in the woods. Later, she is able to recognise him as a grown man by describing to him the clothing in which she left him, clothing which she wove with her own hands. The remembered textile speaks to her of a language she had written long ago, one that she alone can read:

This shawl was all I had, girl as I was,
To wrap you in – a thing I made playing with my loom.
–Euripides, Ion[13]

Remembering someone through the language of fabric, however, is not merely an interesting literary or plot motif. During the American Civil War in the mid 19th century, soldiers whose bodies had drastically decomposed could still be identified by family members: the lining of a coat, sewn by a mother or sisters, was often quilted with a recognisable design made with the family's stash of fabric and bits of cloth. Likewise, in the seafaring tradition of Britain, the wives and sisters of sailors would often knit individual, personalised patterns into traditional sweater designs as a means of identification. Those garments made by hand, carry with them a history that begins with their production and continues through their ownership.

The idea of memory and its relationship to textiles and culture is the subject of Tilleke Schwarz's embroidery *Losing our Memory* [fig. 6]. Her embroidery fuses together elements from a sampler, a computer program, a child's doodling and graffiti. The lower right hand part of the embroidery reveals the disorder of threads often viewed on the back of a tapestry. Through her embroidery Schwarz suggests that all of our texts are in danger of disintegrating because the thread of our communication is more reliant on technology than on human relationships.

The Fabric of Myth addresses many facets of what textiles mean to us. Although many collectors have preferred painting and sculpture, and have often overlooked the significance of textiles (perhaps because of their functional dimension, made primarily for human consumption), it is precisely because of their (sometimes) pedestrian use and the communal context of their production that they deserve to be admired and valued. Whether we wrap ourselves in fabric, hang it on our walls, revere, treasure or inherit it, we are ultimately transformed by it. This exhibition invites us to take hold of Ariadne's thread and with this golden clue follow it through the maze of art, literature and language, and so understand how the collective experiences of our ancestors have shaped and transformed so many aspects of our lives.

1. Lessing, Doris. *The Golden Notebook*. New York, NY: HarperPerrenial, 1999.

2. In another version of this story the woman is 'quilling' a blanket (with porcupine quills).

3. Dated 19 February 1818 from *Letters of John Keats*, selected and edited by Robert Gittings (Oxford, New York: Oxford University Press, 1982): p. 158.

4. Fowler, Brenda. "Find in Europe Suggests that Weaving Preceeded Settled Life," in The *New York Times* (Tuesday, 9 May 1995): C–, C10. Also, see Annette B. Weiner's & Jane Schneider's comprehensive study, *Cloth and Human Experience*, (Washington & London: Smithsonian Institution Press, 1989) as well as Elizabeth Wayland Barber's fascinating *Women's Work, the First 20,000 Years: Women, Cloth and Society in Early Times*, (New York & London: W.W. Norton & Company, 1994). Also, see Scheid, John and Jesper Svenbro. *The Craft of Zeus: Myths of Weaving and Fabric*. Trans. by Carol Volk (Cambridge, Massachusetts and London, England: Harvard University Press, 1996).

5. See Eva Keuls's essay, "Attic Vase-Painting and the Home Textile Industry." *Ancient Greek Art and Iconography*. Ed. Warren G. Moon. (Madison, Wisconsin: University of Wisconsin Press, 1983): pp. 209–30.

6. See Ann Bergren's article "Language and the Female in Early Greek Thought," in *Arethusa 16* (1983): 6–95. Bergren traces the concept of mētis "or transformative intelligence" (71) to the goddess Mētis, swallowed by Zeus after their marriage.

7. *The Odyssey of Homer*. Trans. by Richmond Lattimore. New York, NY: HarperPerrenial, 1991. All subsequent quotes refer to this translation.

8. Walker, Susan. "Women and Housing in Classical Greece: the Archaeological Evidence," in *Images of Women in Antiquity*. Ed. Averil Cameron and Amelie Kuhrt (Detroit: Wayne State University Press, 1983).

9. Ovid. *The Metamorphosis*. Trans. by A. D. Melville. Oxford, New York: Oxford University Press, 1986, p.166. All subsequent quotes refer to this translation.

10. Vogh, James. *Arachne Rising: the Search for the Thirteenth Sign of the Zodiac* (New York: Dial Press, 1977): pp. 75–95. Also, J.E. Cirlot, *Dictionary of Symbols*. (London: Routledge & Kegan Paul, 1962): p. 209.

11. One of the best known essays on this topic is Susan Gubar's " 'The Blank Page' and the Issues of Female Creativity." *Critical Inquiry* 8 (Winter 1981): pp. 243–65.

12. For a closer study of Greek's legendary weavers, see my book, *Weaving the Word: the Metaphorics of Weaving and Female Textual Production*. (Selinsgrove and London: Susquehanna University Press / Associated University Presses, 2001).

13. Euripides. *Ion, The Bacchae and Other Plays*. Trans. by Philip Vellacott (London, England: Penguin, 1972): p. 84.

Fig. 7 *Penelope Surprised by the Suitors (detail)* [31]

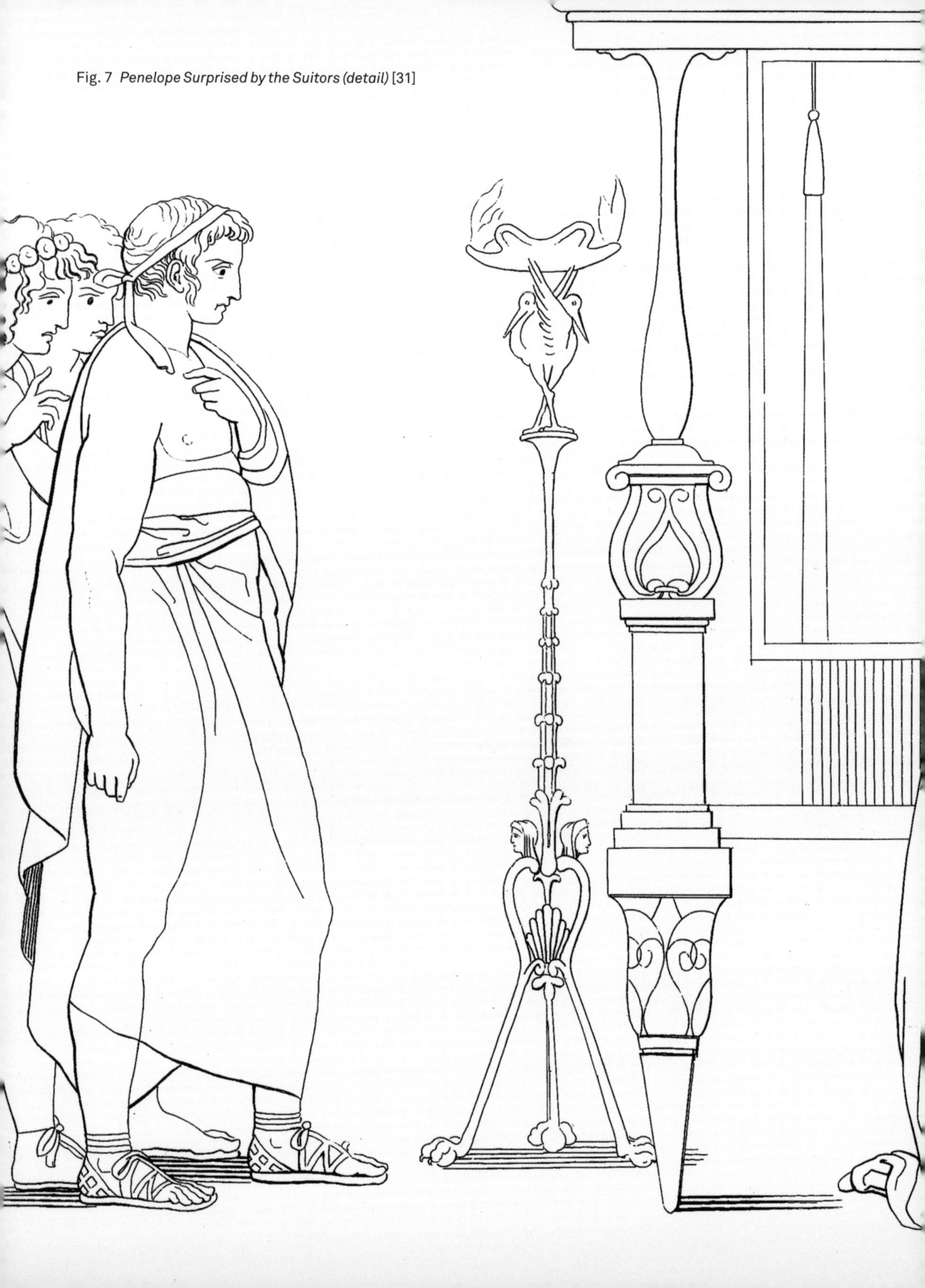

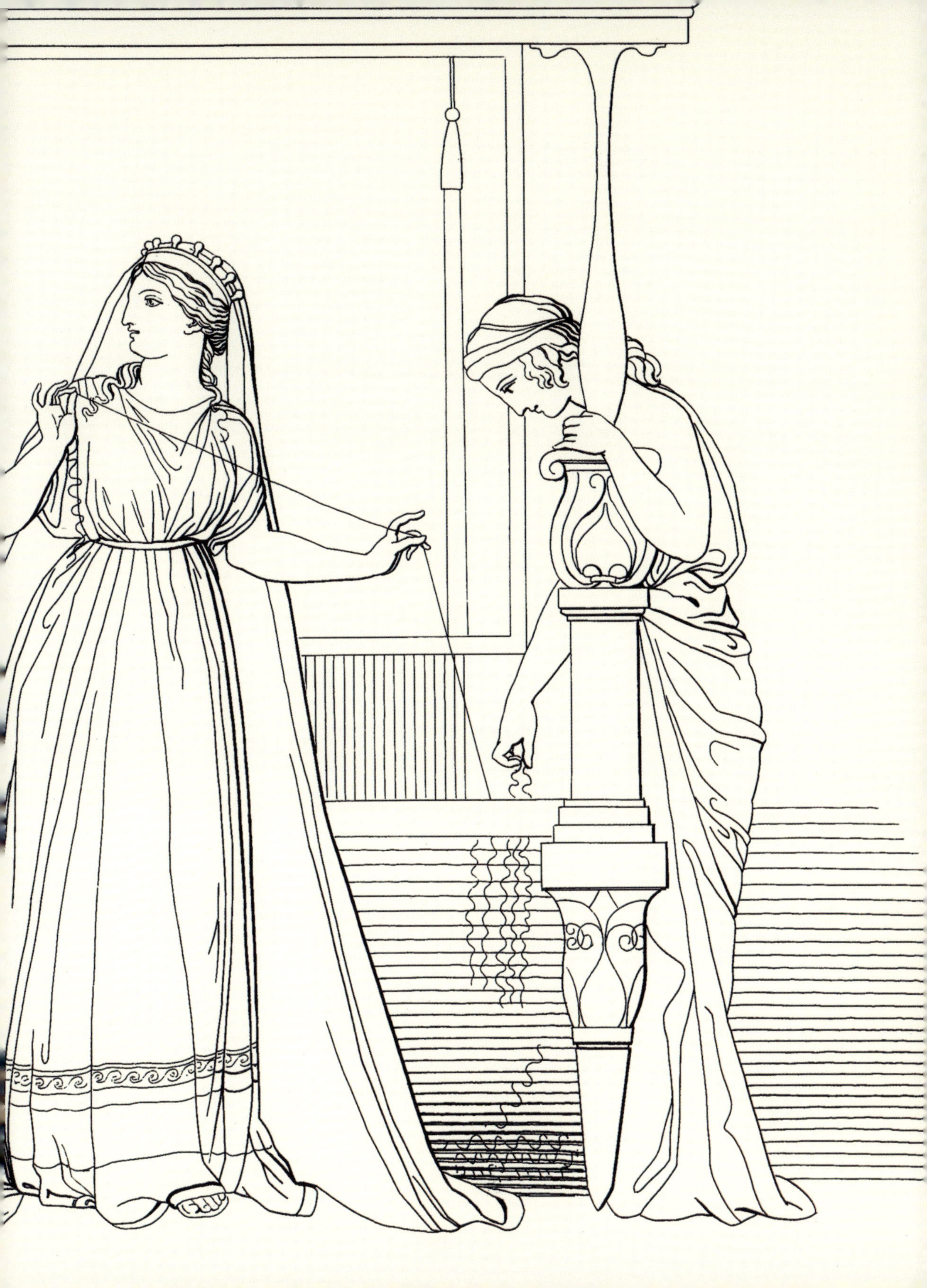

Weaving, unweaving and reweaving: the legacy of Penelope

Antonia Harrison

From which it seems to follow that the business of thinking
is like the veil of Penelope: it undoes every morning
what it had finished the night before.
–Hannah Arendt, Thinking and Moral Considerations[1]

Homer's *The Odyssey* gives us various accounts of Penelope's strategy to weave, unweave and reweave the shroud of her father-in-law, Laertes. This act buys her time until the return of her husband, Odysseus, from the Trojan War by warding off the many suitors who wish to take his place. One of these suitors, Amphimedon, describes the final woven shroud as gleaming 'like the sun or moon'.[2] This description mirrors the method of the shroud's production, woven by day and unravelled by night, as if the very fabric itself has become imbued with the circumstances of its creation. Moreover, it is the volition of the creative act which brings about the change to Penelope's destiny, as if the threads have taken on their own future course of action and thought has become something tangible and visible.

Ultimately, Penelope is forced to finish the shroud after a maidservant witnesses her undoing of the work, and alerts

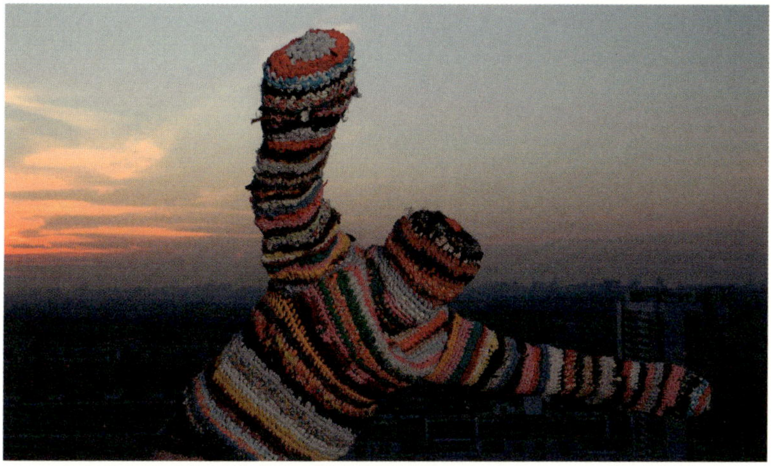

Fig. 8 Leonid Tishkov *The Vyazanik (The Knitling)* [33]

the suitors to her deception [fig. 7]. The shroud can therefore be seen to represent both a harnessing of power and a loss of control, at the same time as it represents both time passing and time standing still.

The artist Leonid Tishkov has explored such a reciprocal relationship between fabric and time passing in *The Vyazanik* (*The Knitling*) [fig. 8]. Inspired by his ancestral history, Tishkov asked his mother to unravel and then re-work the garments of his family's past into one all-encompassing, crocheted swaddling suit. Each band of fabric conveys a personal narrative which is written alongside, and an accompanying film documents its making.

The suit is anchored in the tradition of the Urals, Tishkov's homeland, for knitting rugs out of hand-me-downs to preserve the memory of the deceased and protect their kinsfolk. *The Knitling* acts as a cocoon of memory which, when worn, transports the artist into a timeless world of family ties and cultural traditions. The suit has been transformed by its method of production into what the artist refers to as 'a new mythical creature'.

The Knitling also includes a group photo of the artist's relations staring out at us, which in contrast to the suit itself, seems to highlight how disconnected a photograph can seem from the subjects it captures. The artist himself appears as a young boy in the centre of the group surrounded by his relations. *The Knitling* has become the literal embodiment of this early familial protection. In the accompanying film, Tishkov's mother can be seen unravelling and reworking these endless bands of

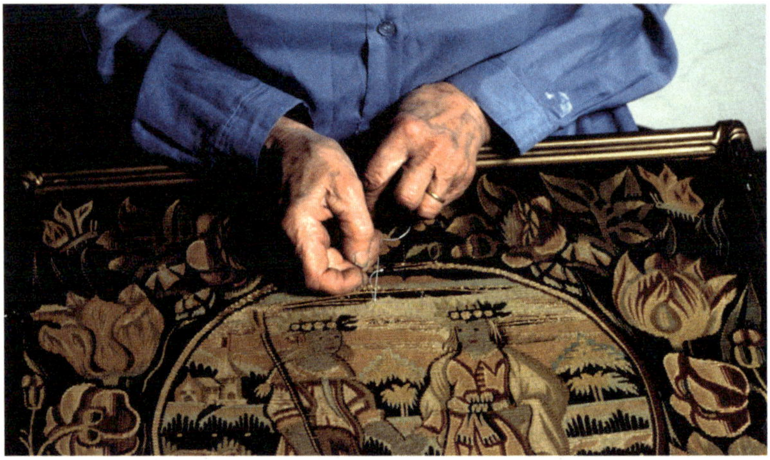

Fig. 9 *Louise Bourgeois restoring a tapestry fragment*

memory in the manner of a latter day Penelope, talking us through them as if they were a family album.

Louise Bourgeois' relationship to fabric, and its process of creation with needle and thread, can also be seen to summon up memories and familial history. Bourgeois' family worked in the Aubusson tapestry industry in France, her mother being a tapestry weaver and restorer. From a young age Bourgeois herself carried out the repairs and redesign of antique tapestries in the family workshop. She has recalled the tapestries hanging in the family home as being like moveable walls, a pliable architecture which she and her siblings would hide amongst.[3] These formative experiences shaped her artistic career. The needle and thread from her past have been used to create a large body of fabric sculptures and the themes of sewing, spinning and weaving can be seen to be carried through much of her work's conceptual ideology.[4]

Bourgeois' *Needle (Fuseau)* [3] symbolically links her past with her own creativity. The neeedle's dramatic armature and flax ready to be drawn out, spun and stitched, suggest future possibilities and the potential to restore and remake in the manner of Penelope.[5] This act of restoration is driven by her own personal narrative, where she says her sewing has become 'a symbolic action against the fear of being separated and abandoned'.[6] Thus the needle becomes a statue to memory; the flax a latent thread leading back to childhood.

Bourgeois has also made a link between her own work and that of the Brazilian artist Arthur Bispo Do Rosário. Much of Bispo's life was spent institutionalised, although this confinement became the unrestrained backdrop for creative production. A body of work exists of more than eight hundred objects: eight hundred responses to the world around him, a catalogue of his life. A number of works are embroidered, some with the blue threads from his institution uniforms – unravelled and reused. Of Bispo, Bourgeois has said:

> *'One senses in Bispo Do Rosário's work that he too is afraid of losing contact. Like Penelope and the spider, he has spent his whole life doing and undoing. He was seeking an order to the chaos, a structure and rhythm to time and thought.'*[7]

Just as Penelope's desire to weave is generated through her conviction to change the world around her, so too is Bispo's creative process fuelled by a desire to refashion and construct a personal meta-universe. *Manto da Apresentação* (translated *Presentation Cape*) [27], often worn by Bispo during his lifetime, brings together his life's work in one embroidered jacket: a summation of this universe, with himself at the centre. Bispo's embroidery can therefore be seen to trigger memory by the act of creating itself.

Shane Waltener's *Destiny* [29] articulates this territory of production. Threads which spell out the word of the title span a space between two chairs, the now empty seats of the protagonists needed for the creation of the work. While referencing the destiny of Penelope and the Three Fates of Greek mythology, who allot the lifespan of both mortals and

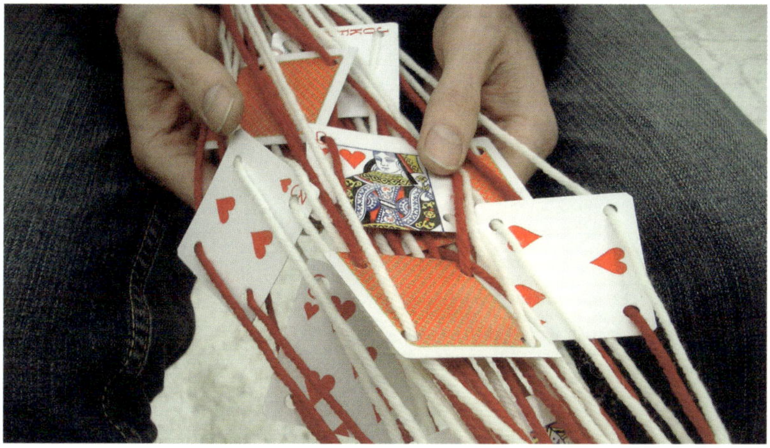

Fig. 10 Shane Waltener working on *Destiny*

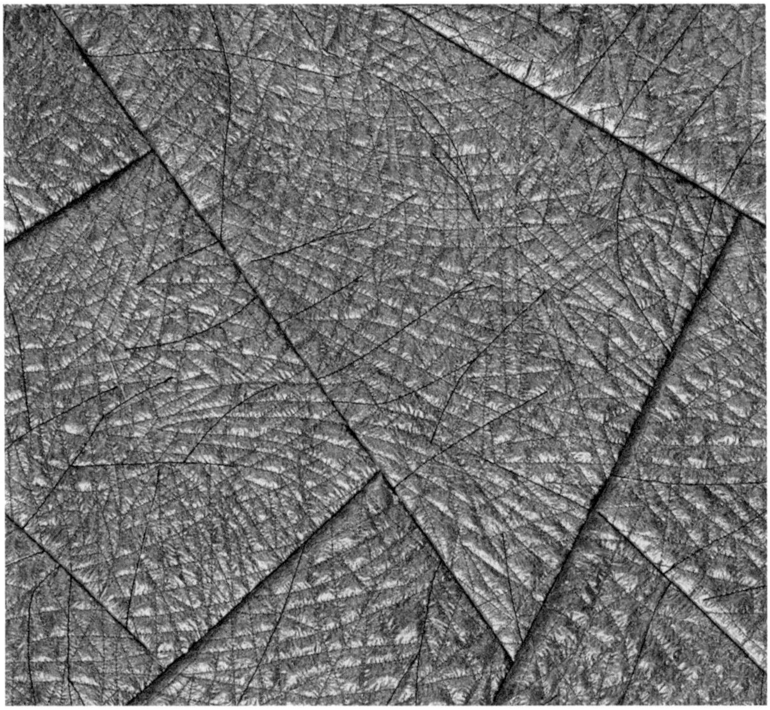

Fig. 11 Michele Walker *Memoriam (detail)* [36]

gods by apportioning lengths of thread, the work draws us into the imagined actions of its makers, and the echoes of their destiny which they are now living out.

Destiny also carries with it echoes of the ancient method of tablet weaving. By attaching yarn to a set of cards or flat tablets, a loom is made, and when these cards are rotated, a woven band is formed. This method of weaving stretches back over two thousand years through North Africa, Europe and Asia. Practised by people including nomadic tribes in Turkey, Burmese monks and medieval ladies at court, this lineage weaves its own path through religious vestments, national costumes and inscribed love tokens. The simplicity of the technique is often lost in the density and intricacies of the finished piece, as if the final message or intent has overtaken its production.

As a process, textile production takes time. The repetition of its making draws in time and opens up a space for remembering. As an articulation of memory, Michele Walkers' *Memoriam* brings together two traditions in its conception – that of the whole cloth method of quilt-making and the notion of memory involved in the making of textiles.

Memoriam [fig. 11] references the artist's mother and her struggle with Alzheimer's disease. *Memoriam* is sewn with the imprint of the artist's own skin through layers of clear plastic and wire wool. The trace of the imprint appears in a metallic grey, the antithesis of skin in both colour and texture, and therefore suggestive of the fading of memory and a transition from the known to the unknown. The use of unconventional materials to produce a quilt subverts the traditional and comforting functionality such an object would usually represent. The quilt that would normally be passed down through generations retaining memory, has instead become a shrine to its loss.

Penelope's weaving and unweaving of Laertes' shroud is itself an act of retaining memory. When she weaves she not only knots threads, but symbolically knots herself to her husband – and in turn to his destiny. In an act that is at once defiant of her current situation she also challenges the Fates, whose spinning Homer recounts in relation to Odysseus' destiny:

> *...but there in the future*
> *he shall endure all that his destiny and the heavy Spinners*
> *spun for him with the thread at his birth...*[8]

In this way Penelope's weaving can be reduced to a thread which stretches out in a seamless time continuum. The weaving and unweaving looks back to the thread of life at Odysseus' birth, and forward to a future destiny.

1. Hannah Arendt, *Thinking and Moral Considerations*, Social Research 38 (1971), p.425
2. Homer, *The Odyssey*, Penguin, 2003, Chapter 24, pp. 147–48
3. Louise Bourgeois quoted in Frances Morris, *Stitches in Time*, AugustProjects, IMMA, MOCA, 2003, p.25
4. Ibid., p. 22
5. Marina Warner, *Nine Turns around the Spindle: The Turbine Towers of Louise Bourgeois*, in Louise Bourgeois, London: Tate, 2000
6. Arthur Bispo Do Rosário, Published by Museu Bispo Do Rosário Arte Contemporânea, 2006, Louise Bourgeois introductory quote, p.22
7. Ibid., p.22
8. Homer, *The Odyssey*, trans by Richmond Lattimore, New York NY: Harper Perrenial, 1991, Penguin, Chapter 7, pp. 196–98

I would like to acknowledge Marina Warner's writing in *Nine Turns around the Spindle: The Turbine Towers of Louise Bourgeois* (Tate, 2000) and her writing and ideas on myth and metamorphosis

Clothbound: Revelations in Restraint and the Weaver's Art

James Young

It wraps us at our entrance to and exit from this world. It protects and insulates us from the elements. It covers and colours our lives yet its presence has, in some sense, faded.

Textile was a primary product of the industrial revolution. Until the invention of the spinning jenny and the power loom, the process of making cloth had remained largely unchanged since the Classical Age. Even so, until a generation or so ago, garments were repaired by hand, by us. Cheap high-street imports now mean that textile has reached a state of disposability closer to that of, say, paper.

Before the growth of the cotton and wool mills of Lancashire and Yorkshire, the making of fabric was a slow and personal process. Whether a peasant's smock or a Queen's robe, a tablecloth or a tapestry, the arts of needlework were skills that all women possessed – and many men. The sailor had to repair clothing and rigging. The soldier had to repair a uniform for campaigns that might take him far from home.

Our relationship to textile, therefore, has shifted since the beginning of that industrial age. Before the industrial era, textile took time. Now we see textile and time differently.

A significant part of *The Fabric of Myth* is devoted to work created in confinement by people forced to have time on their hands. Those on the inside don't have access to the same resources as the people on the other side of the wall. The choice of artistic media is severely restricted. A ball of thread becomes more than the equivalent of a tube of paint. The latter can be bought from a shop. The thread must be begged for, traded, hustled, recycled. The thread and its story become as real as the life.

ITHACA, GREECE. 8TH CENTURY B.C.

A Queen works at her loom, creating a burial shroud for her husband's father. Her handiwork will adorn the departed king on his journey into the realm of the immortals. The weaver is Penelope, the wife of King Odysseus who has gone to fight in the Trojan War. It will be two decades before her husband's return. Confined to the women's quarters, she is at the mercy of a series of ardent suitors:

As a lion ringed by a band of hunters...
–Homer, The Odyssey IV[1]

Penelope devises the strategy of weaving old King Laertes' shroud by day and unpicking it by night. Only when her work is finished will she choose a suitor. Her work is constant, yet the effect is one of suspended animation. Her name, an acronym of 'pene' (web) and 'ops' (eye), suggests an insight into her problem and the tools at her disposal. More than art or craft, this is the performance piece of a lifetime. With it she will save her virtue and the patriarchal line, both of which are of paramount importance to a clan society.

MAXIMUM SECURITY BLOCK, CONNECTICUT CORRECTIONAL INSTITUTION USA, AUTUMN 1988

'I don't mess with nobody and I don't want nobody messing with me.'

Ray Materson has been sent down for twenty-five years for possession and distribution of narcotics, aggravated by an escape attempt, kidnapping and armed robbery (with a fake gun).

'I don't mess with nobody...' Prison reduces a human being to the most primal state. The importance of carving out personal territory within a proscribed and patrolled area is essential to both physical and psychic preservation. The institution is there to eradicate the individual either by putting him to death in the electric chair, just a few yards down from Ray's cell-block, or by slowly eroding any sense of hope and possibility of redemption.

'I don't mess with nobody…' A prisoner has to establish very quickly his own identity and his own parameters among his fellow inmates. 'Doing time' for many prisoners means doing nothing. The prisoner who occupies himself with creative work is engaged in an act of defiance… not simply against authority but against time.

A couple of cells down from Ray, a pair of blue and yellow striped socks are dangling from a top bunk. He cuts a deal with their bemused owner. A pack of smokes for the socks… a steep price.

At moments of epiphany, time collapses, past and present combine to generate future possibility. A grandmother is remembered embroidering on a sewing hoop and so the lid of a plastic coffee container is transformed; a needle is procured from a co-operative guard; a pair of socks is unravelled.

In a maximum-security prison, a prisoner lives in a state of maximum insecurity. 'Embroidery…contraband.' says the supervising captain. But a scrap of cloth can be hidden… a judicious precaution in the context of such a highly charged, high testosterone environment, where a piece of embroidery is potentially a suicide note. And so a metamorphosis into a new life begins by examining and reworking the threads of the old one. Images emerge on the small hoop: a distant father, a first cigarette, a shot of cocaine, the shadow of prison bars, a woman, a chrysalis, re-emergence [18–23]

TUTBURY CASTLE, ENGLAND. MARCH 1569.

'This Queen contriveth daily to resort to my wife's chamber where… she useth to sit working with the needle in which she much delighteth and in devising works.'
–George Talbot, Earl of Shrewsbury

The 'Queen' is Mary Queen of Scots and the 'wife' is Elizabeth 'Bess' of Hardwick. All queens have a mythic status, an imprisoned queen especially. Under relentless scrutiny

Fig. 12 Ray Materson *Tiny: Life×6, The Noon Watch J2 (detail)* [21]

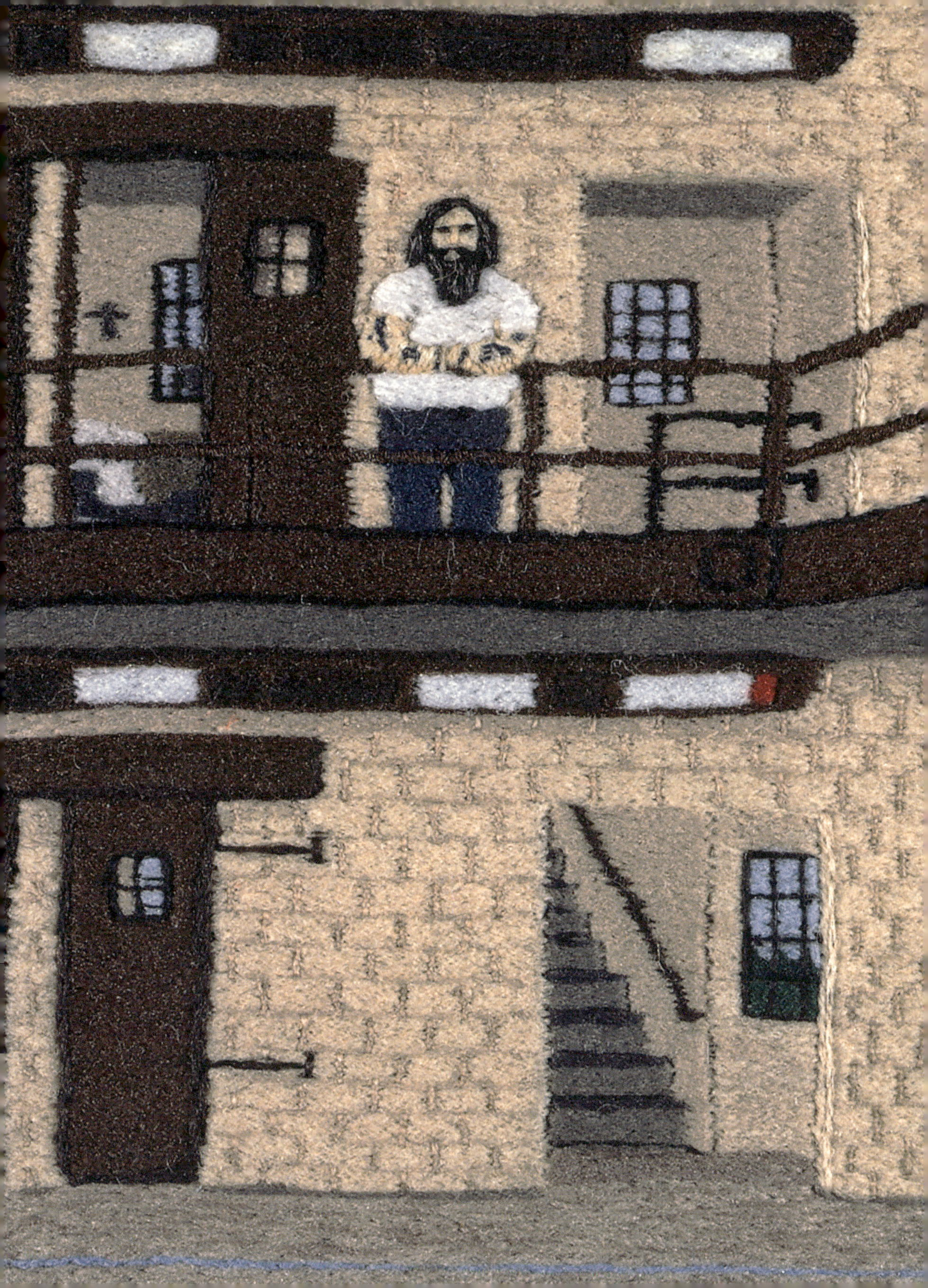

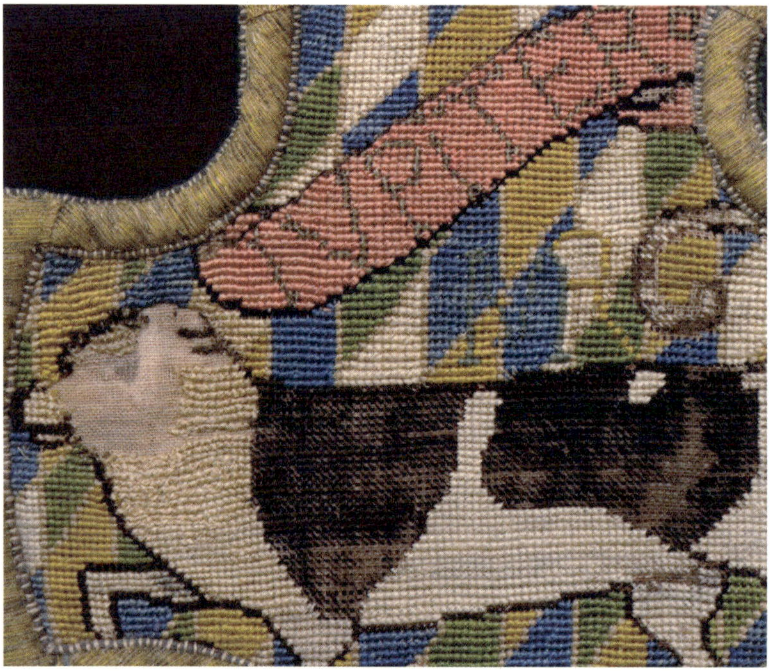

Fig. 13 Mary Queen of Scots *The Oxburgh Hangings, Dog Motif (detail)* [17]

from Bess and her husband, Mary must resort to subterfuge to convey the ignominy of her position. Emblem books are plundered for designs, cryptograms invented, mottoes loaded with extra meaning. Begging for materials, Mary supervises an intense level of embroidery production, a constant stream of communication in stitch. The urgency of her situation and the time-consuming detail of her medium invest Mary's work with a mythic resonance. Even now when we see these sometimes threadbare silks we still feel an acute intelligence at work.

From the time of her first imprisonment in 1567 on the island of Lochleven, until her execution in 1587 at Fotheringay, Mary is obliged to live in as many as eight different locations. Her fate uncertain, her letter writing severely restricted, she must disguise and dissemble. When Nicholas White, a young envoy from the court of Queen Elizabeth, arrives to make a report, he finds the dethroned Queen of Scots sitting upon a cloth of estate, a heraldic tapestry conveying her rank. It bears the motto of her mother, Marie de Guise: '*En Ma Fin Git Ma Commencement*' (*In My End Is My Beginning*). 'A riddle I understand not', the young man ingenuously reports to Elizabeth… a wise observation to make to an autocrat, sensitive to sedition.

Mary introduced from Europe the fashionable art of needlework to the Hardwick household. The working in coloured thread of a small section of canvas, hand-held, portable, intimate, was an amusing new pastime for ladies of the French Court. It became, in Mary's hands, a language of dissent. Living on borrowed time, Mary did not seek distractions. A learned and imaginative woman (unlike the more pragmatic Bess), Mary amassed a library of texts and images. With such resources she could suggest, with exquisite wit, the nature of her predicament. '*A Catte*' (Oxburgh Hall), an image derived from *Gesner's 'Icones Animalium'* 1560, is reinvented as a ginger cat (Elizabeth was a famous redhead) with a small crown on its head, fixedly staring at a mouse. Animals and plants become subjects of both allegorical and poignant meaning. A yellow rose, withering with canker, denotes despair; dandelion heads convey the passing of time. A moth-eaten and faded panel of a loved dog, 'Jupiter', reaches out across four centuries to bring us close to her [fig.13]. At Mary's execution, a small dog ran out from under her skirts and placed itself between her severed head and torso.

RIO DE JANEIRO, BRAZIL. DECEMBER 1938.

A man in his late twenties, Arthur Bispo Do Rosário, appears in a house in a residential suburb of Rio. Not born of human parents, he is accompanied by seven angels bathed in blue light and is guided by the Virgin Mary whom he calls his mother. His mission is to gather together the things of this world and present them before the Lord on Judgement Day. He is arrested and sent to the psychiatric hospital Colonia Juliano Moreira.

Remaining in the hospital for the next fifty years (and never leaving it for the last twenty-five) Bispo collects the detritus of everyday life... old combs, bottles, cutlery, rubber boots... an endless list of everything and rearranges it in preparation for the new cosmic order. He unravels the blue thread of old hospital uniforms: this will be the ink with which he will write a unique cosmography linked by train journeys, sea voyages, friends, saints and the sacred texts of the new dispensation. Old hospital sheets and blankets are transformed into banners embroidered with memories of his other life as a sailor, boxer and handyman. His ultimate creation, taking decades to complete, is his *Presentation Cape* [fig. 14]. A shamanic robe that also proclaims his Christian belief, it is adorned with

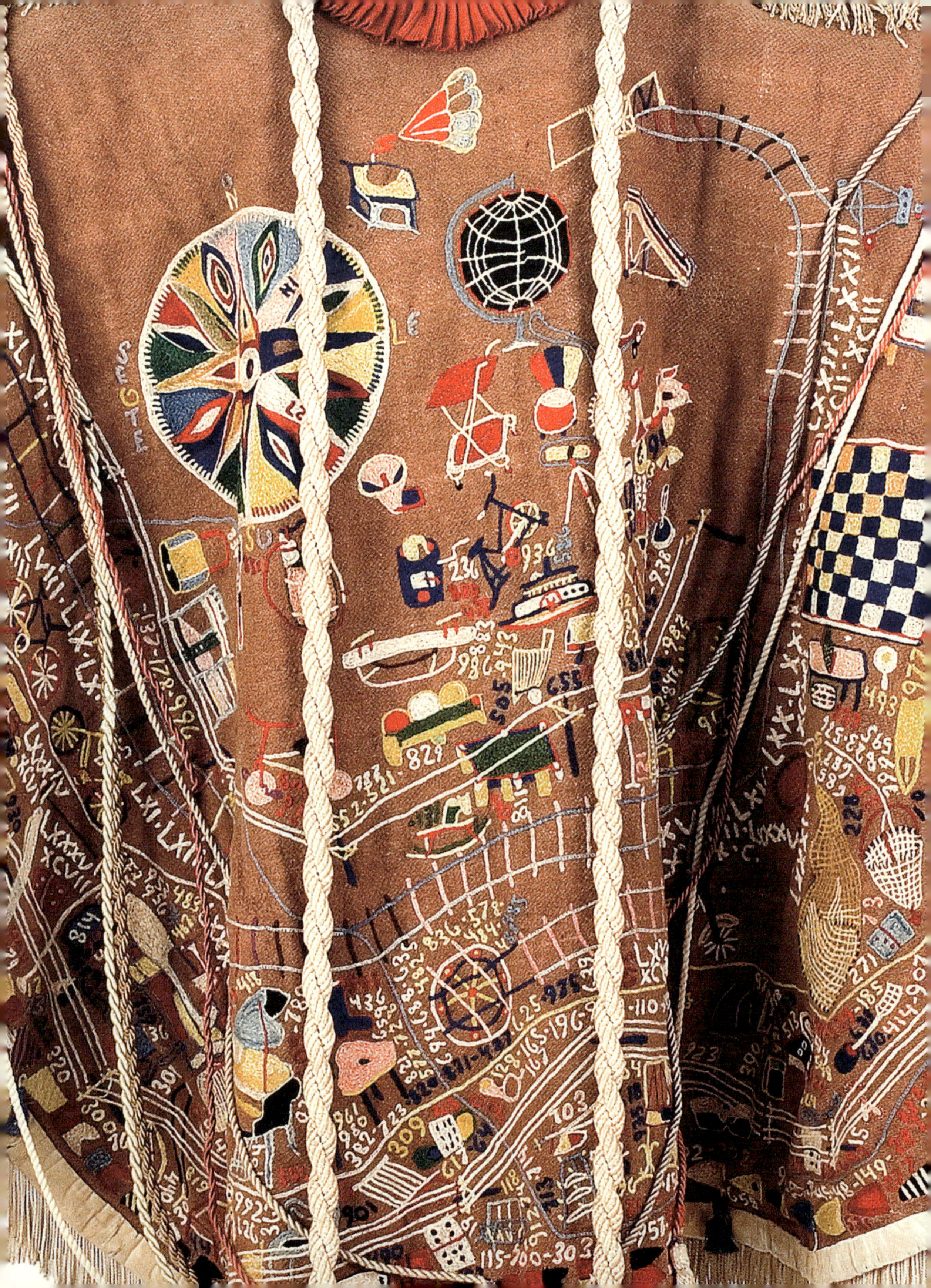

names of all the people he knew in his life, images of places seen and imagined, embroidered versions of objects he created. Bispo will literally wrap the world around himself in his role as a witness for mankind when he stands before the Almighty.

An ascetic, Bispo fasted and spoke little, answering instead what he believed were voices from heaven. To the secular western mind this seems like lunacy. Bispo was a mystic and to the urbane westerner, nurtured by the comforts of clear-sighted progressive thinking, he is an anachronism. But cultures and individuals are not necessarily synchronistic. His apparent lunacy could also be interpreted as a reasonable reaction to an insane urban society.

His studio was a padded cell and his work was not made of marble or bronze, but rags and junk. Even the idea of 'work' seems alien... the pure necessity of Bispo's activity was generated by a spiritual energy. 'Work' often implies something separate from the inner life. Bispo was a total being, he was not engaged in 'doing and undoing' as has been suggested, but the reverse. He is not trapped like Penelope, neither is he commenting on his life... he is living it. He is free of 'art'.

All lives are confined. Even lives of apparent dissipation can be counterbalanced by the solitary rigours of the studio. These examples of the weaver's art are the result of confinement in extreme circumstances: abandonment, imprisonment, dethronement, the end of time. Penelope's fate was to test the meaning of loyalty. Mary Queen of Scots embodied a faith, Catholicism, and a regal responsibility to the present and the future, so that for her each strand of silk weighed heavy. Ray Materson clung to a thread and was pulled out of an abyss. And Bispo Do Rosário wove his way to the stars, ahead of us and on time. The thread connects us.

1. Homer, *The Odyssey,* Trans. Walter Shewring, Oxford University Press, 1980.

Fig. 14 Arthur Bispo Do Rosário *Manto da Apresentação (Presentation Cape) (detail)* [27]

1. *Ariadne and Theseus at the entrance to the Labyrinth*
1563

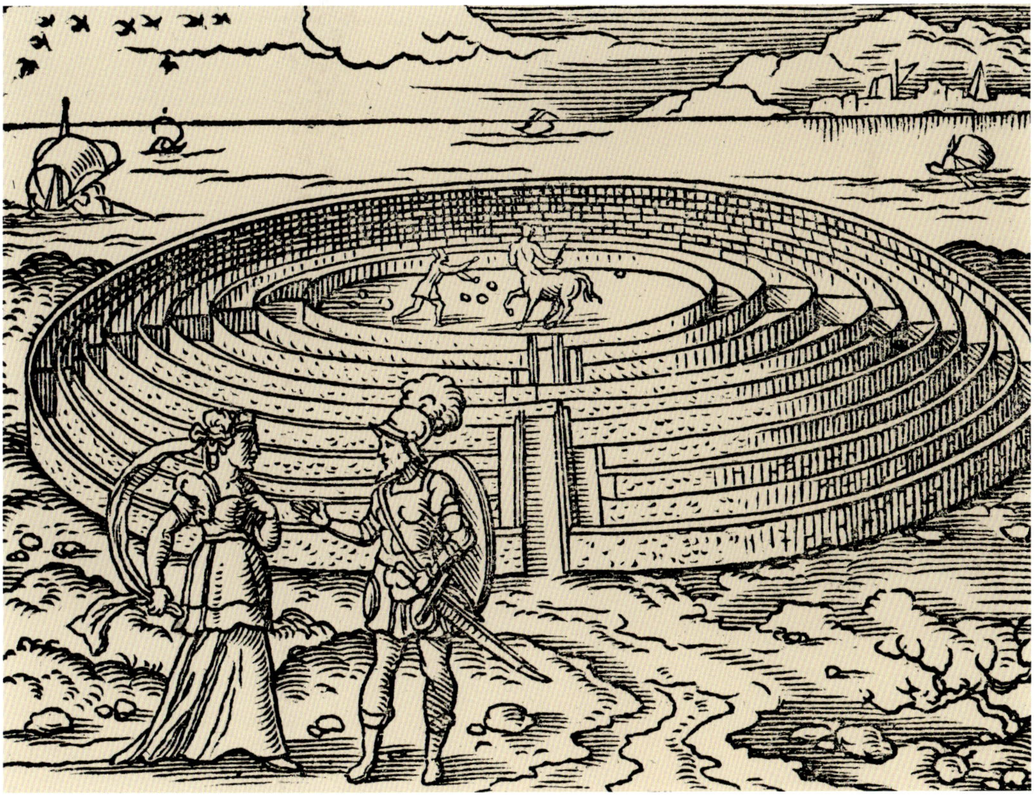

2. *Ariadne*
5th century AD

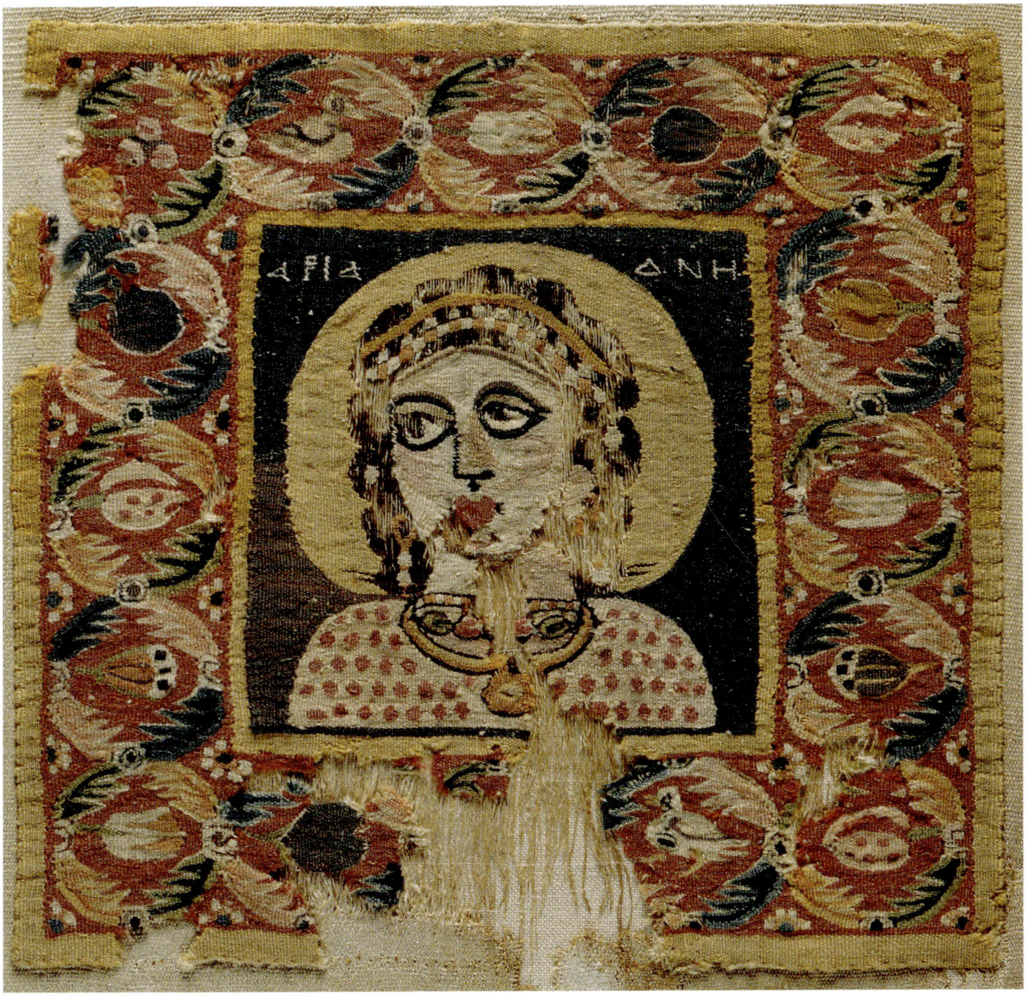
ΑΡΙΑ ΔΝΗ

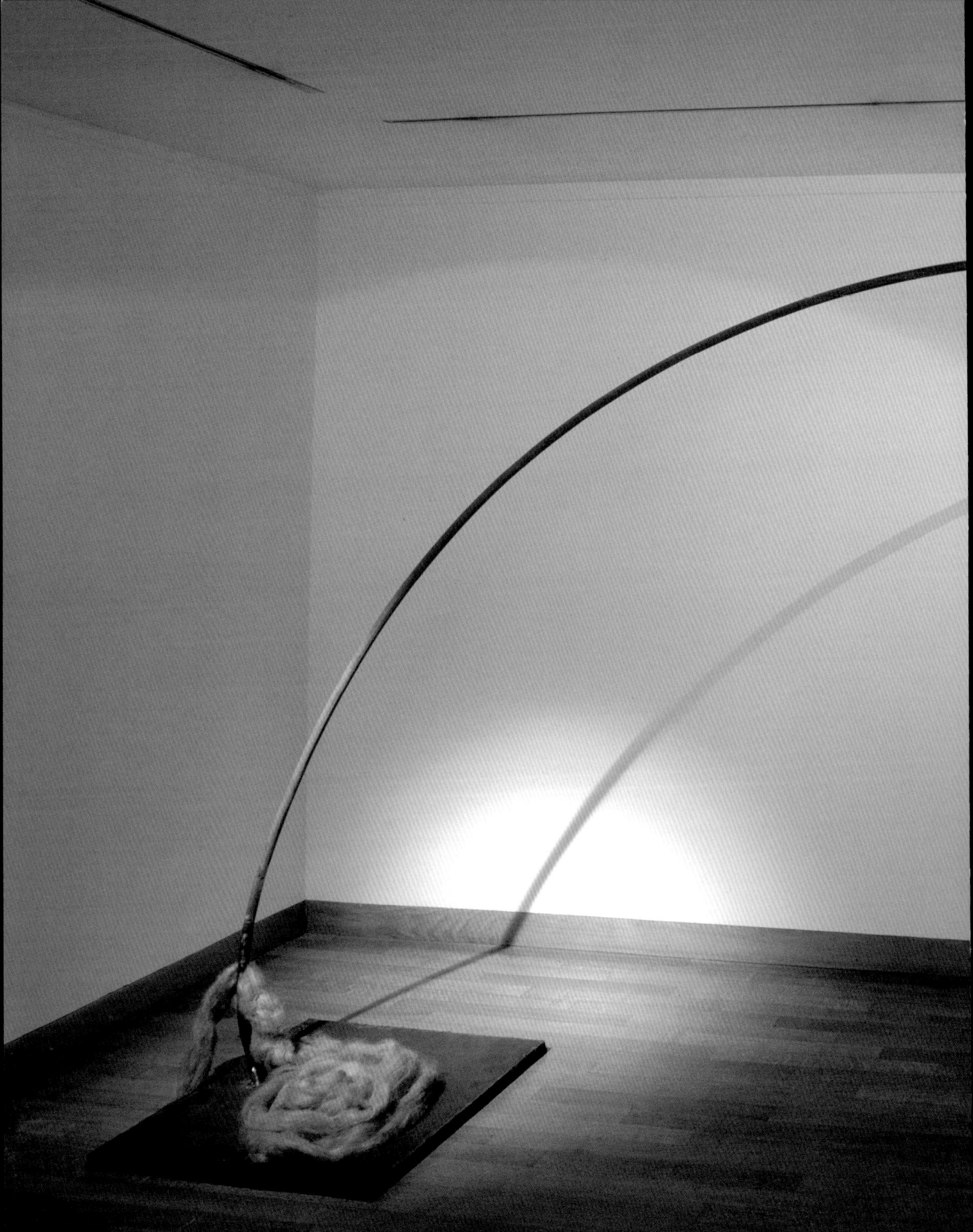

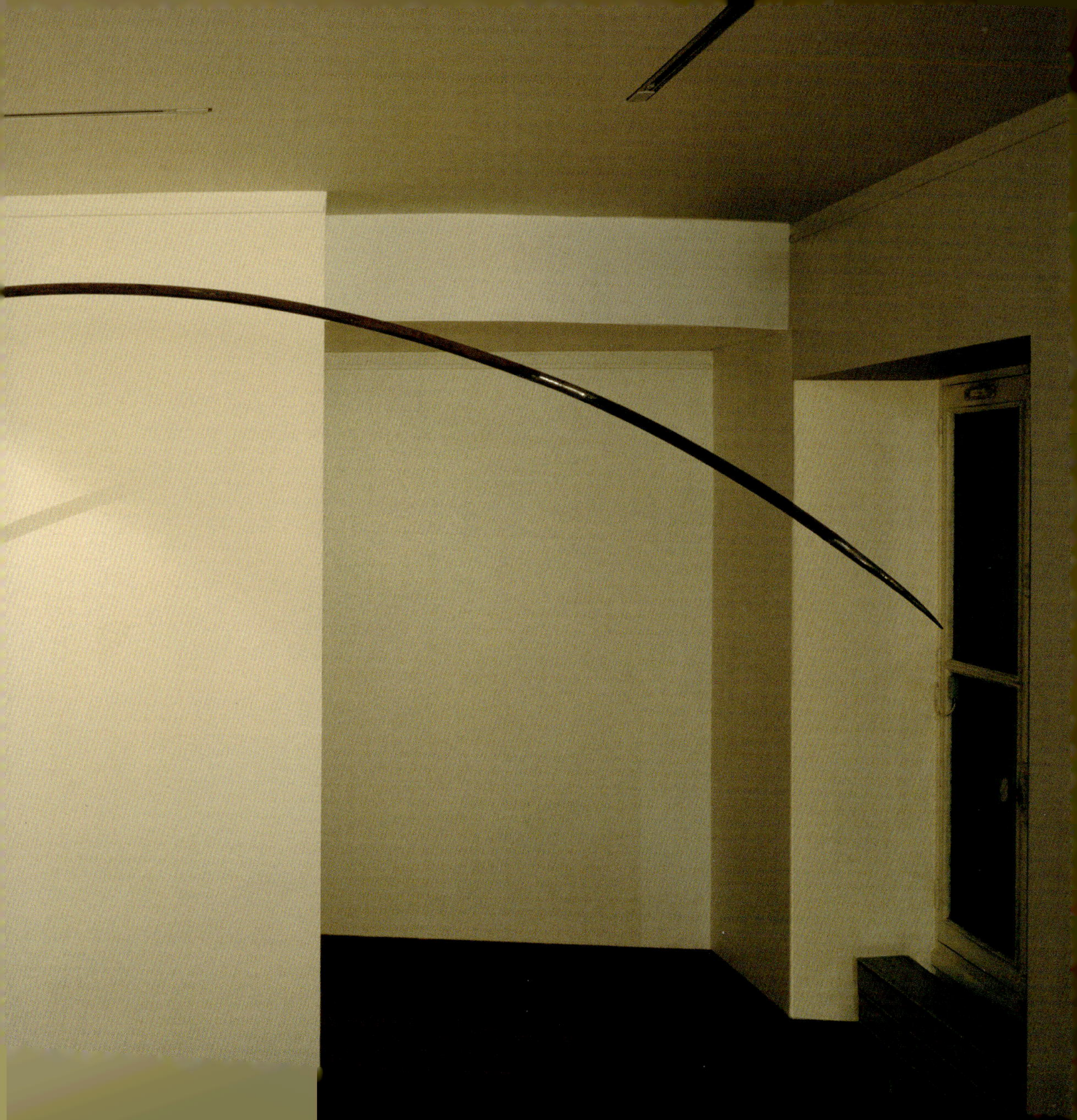

4. *Odysseus and Circe on the island of Aeaea*
c.1550–1600

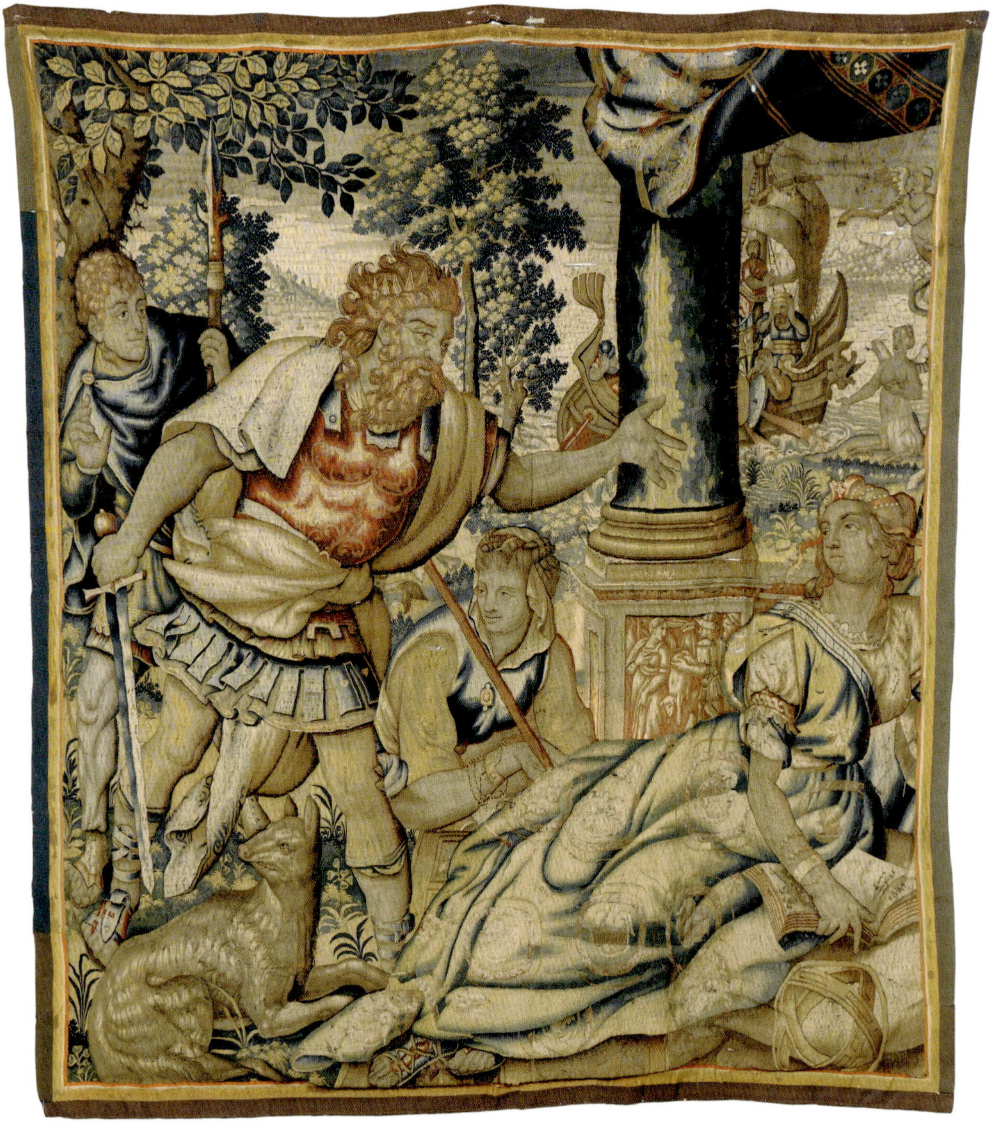

5. *Odysseus and Circe*
4th century BC

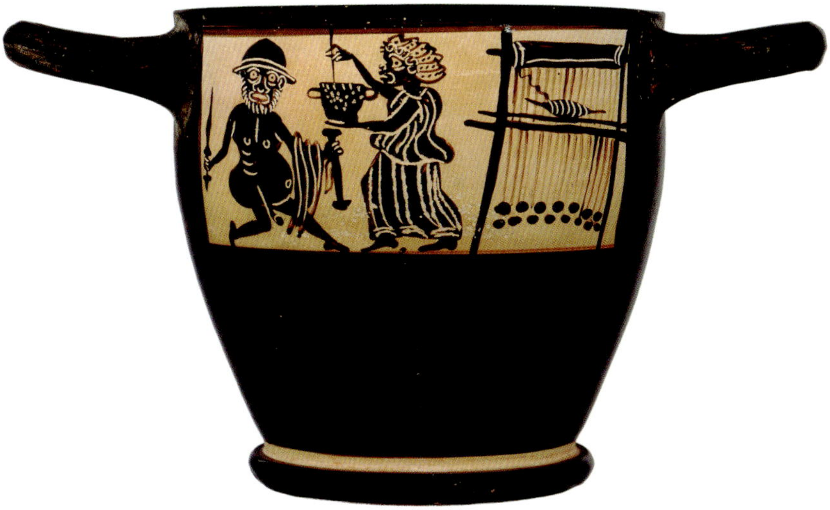

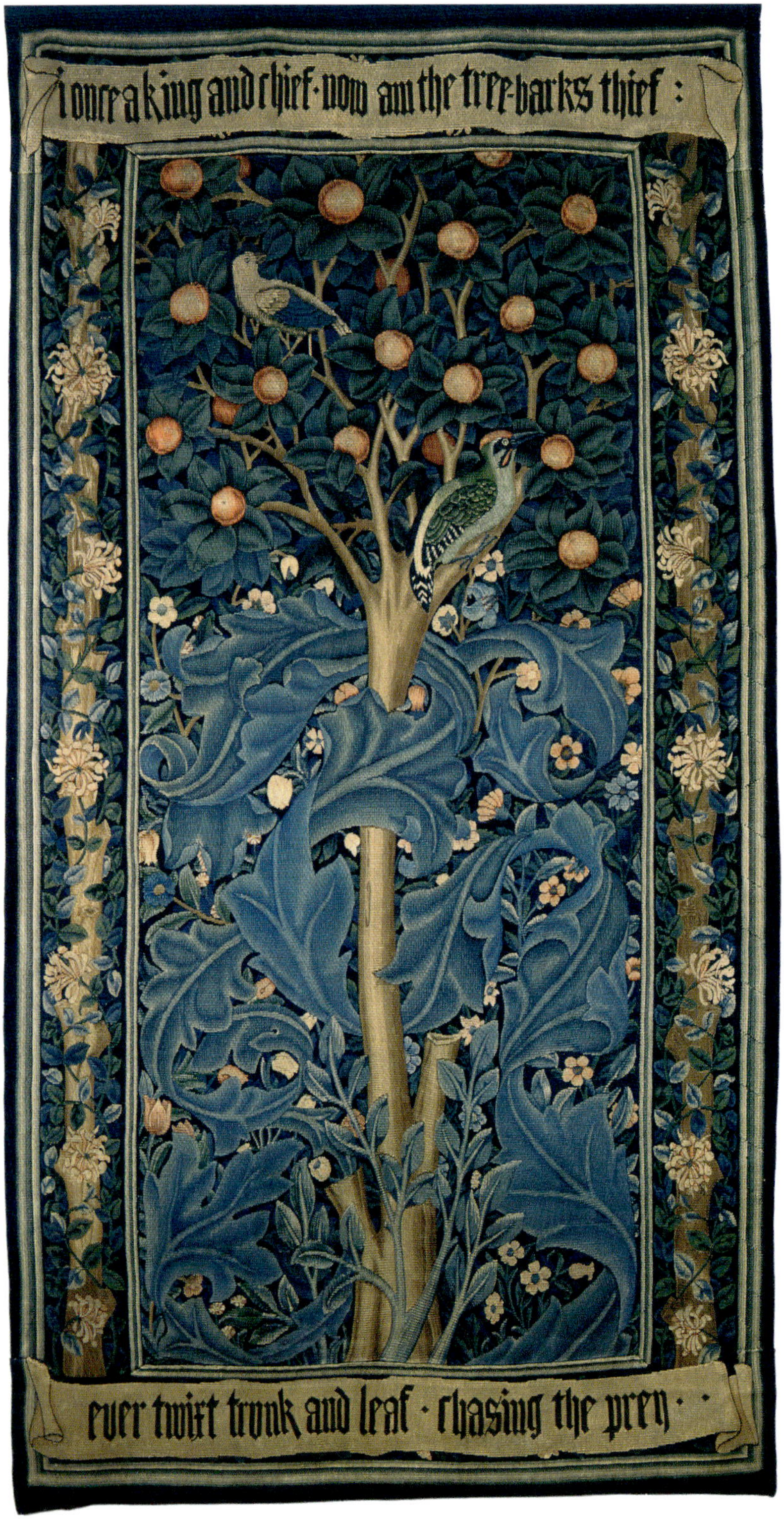
i once a king and chief · now am the tree-barks thief :
ever twixt trunk and leaf · chasing the prey · ·

6. William Morris
The Woodpecker
1885

7. *Europa and the Bull*
1563

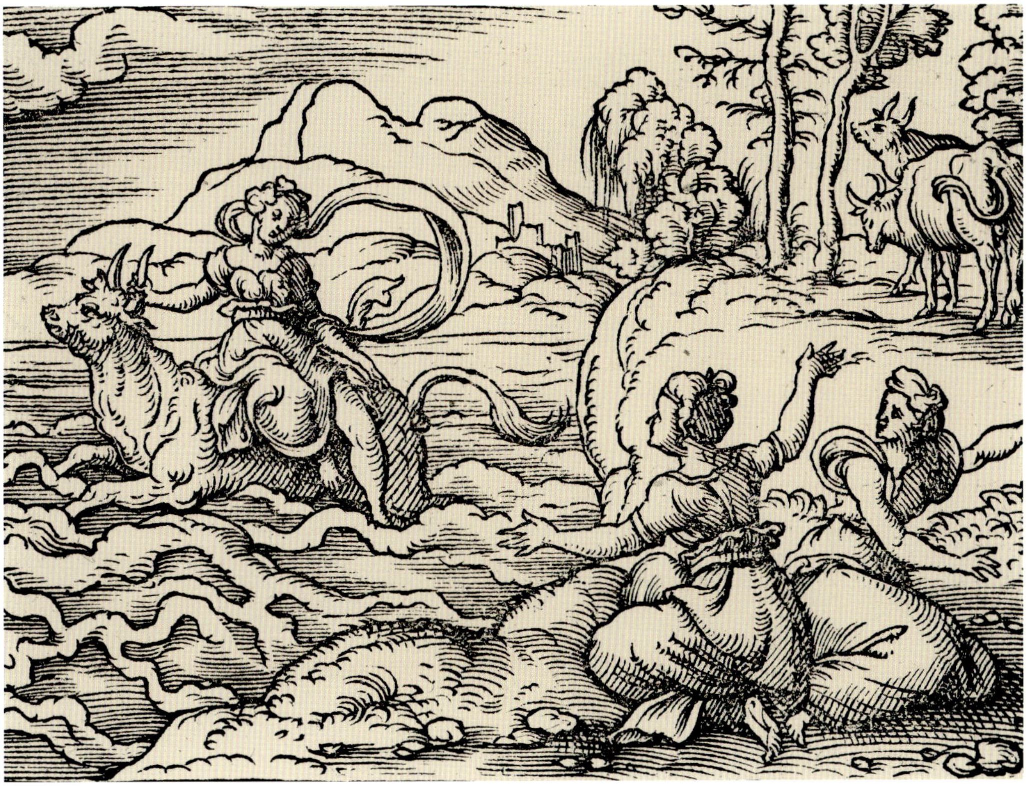

8. Elizabeth Hardwick, Countess of Shrewsbury
Europa and the Bull
c. 1580

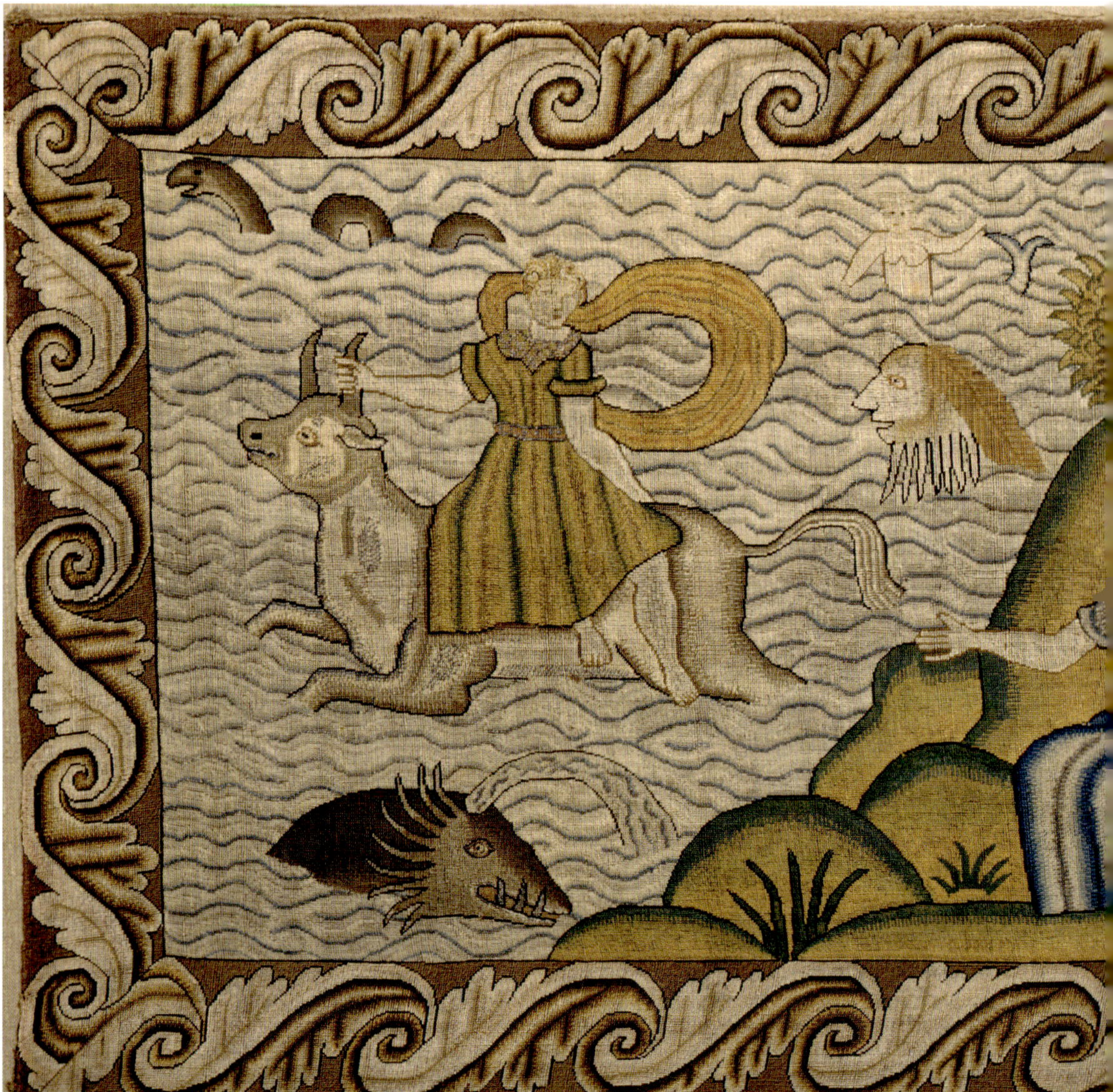

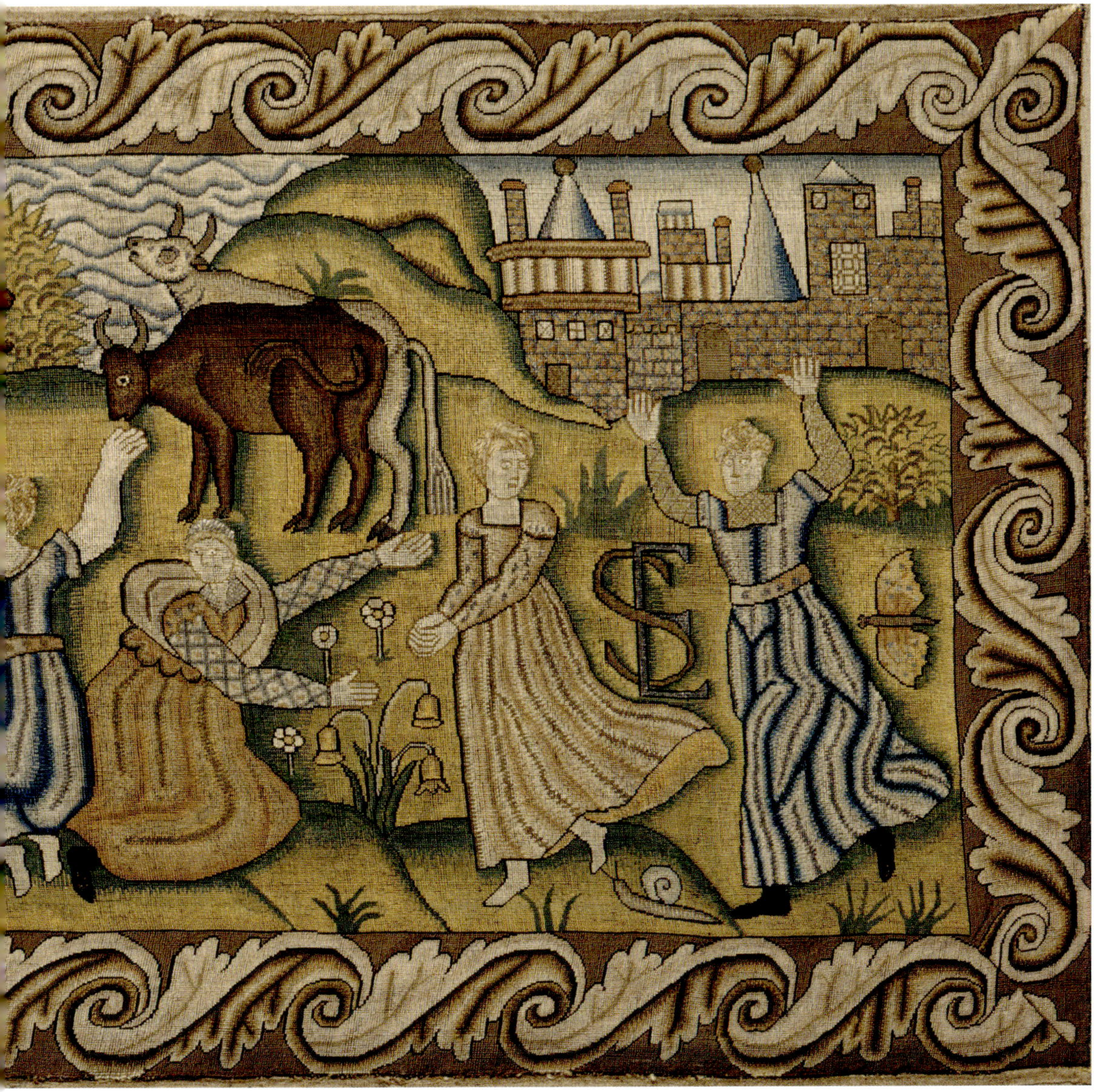

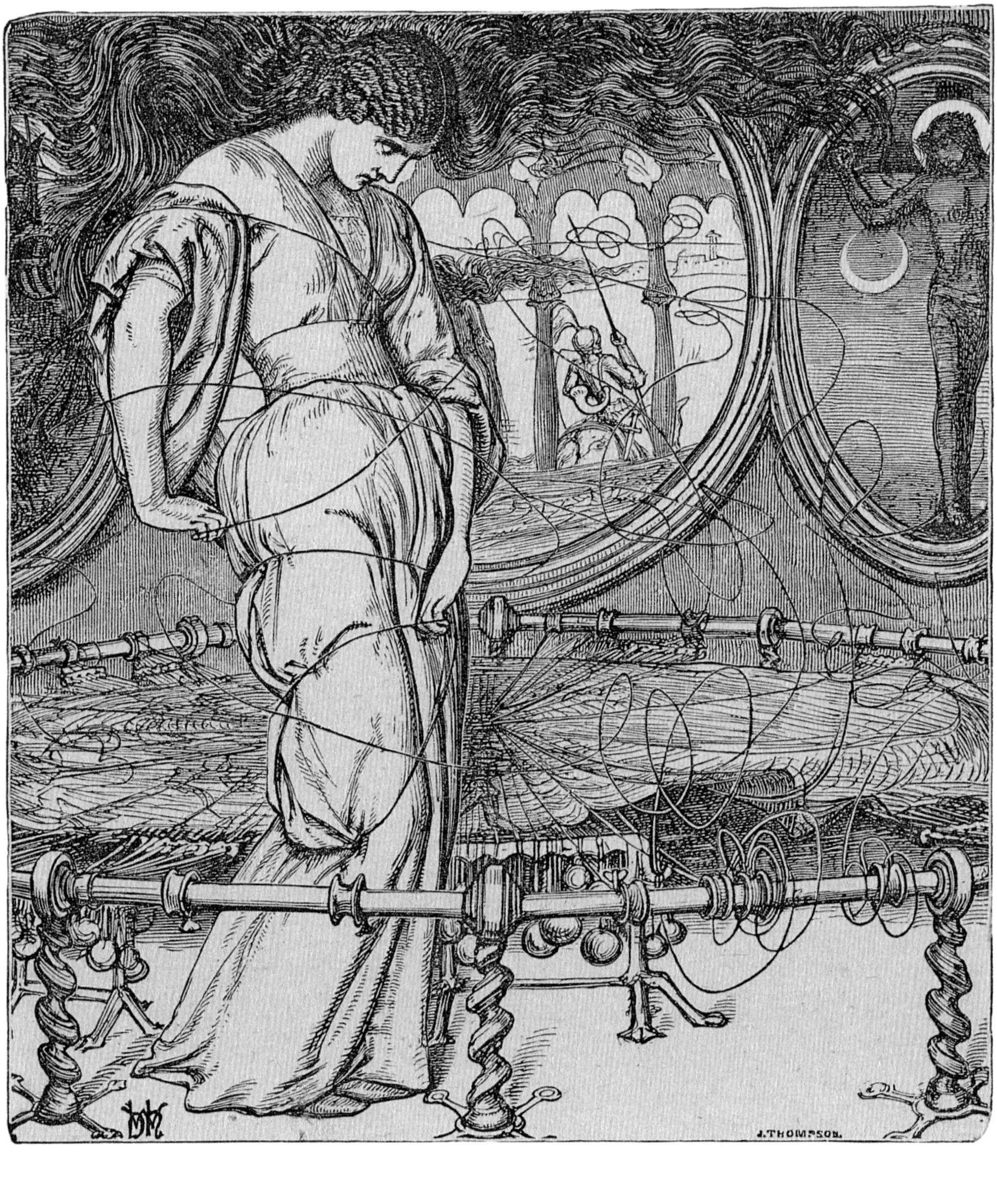
J. THOMPSON

9. William Holman Hunt
The Lady of Shalott
1857

10. Alice Kettle
Metamorphosis
2003

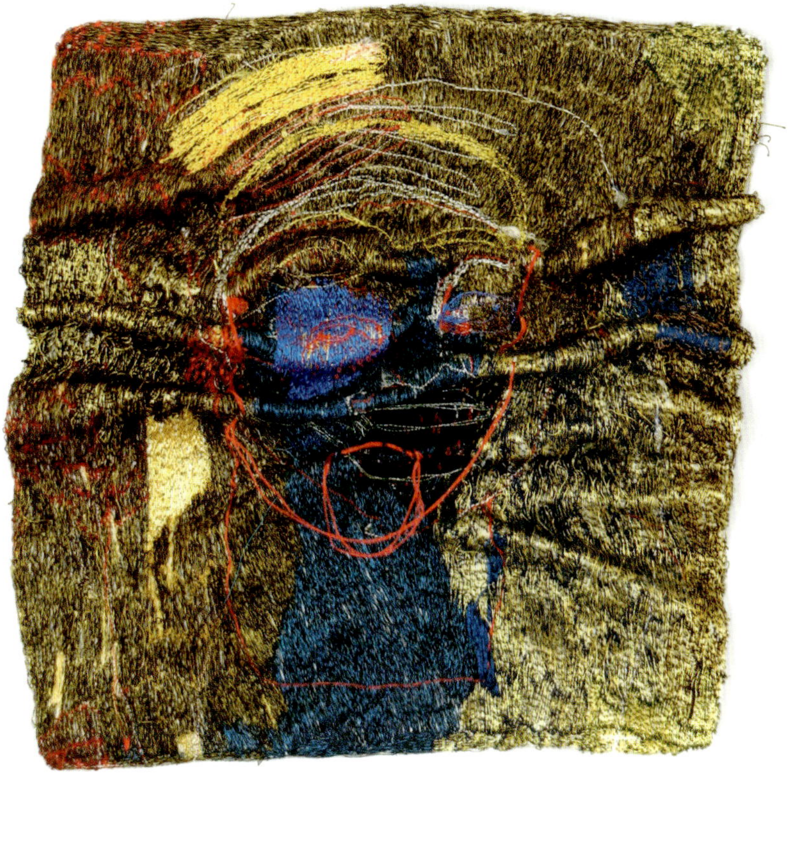

11. *Arachne and Athena weaving contest*
1497

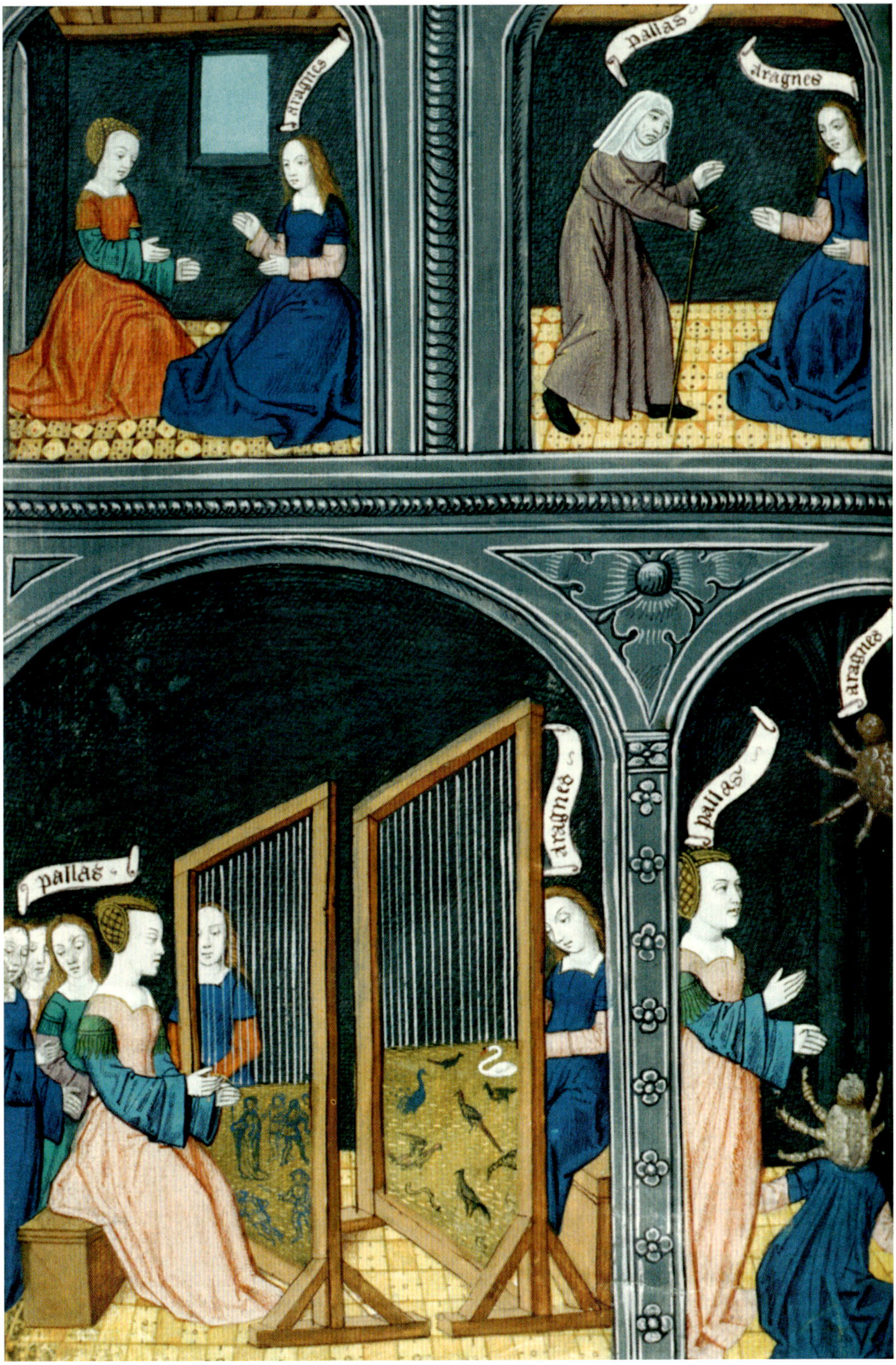
aragnes
pallas
aragnes
pallas
aragnes
pallas
aragnes

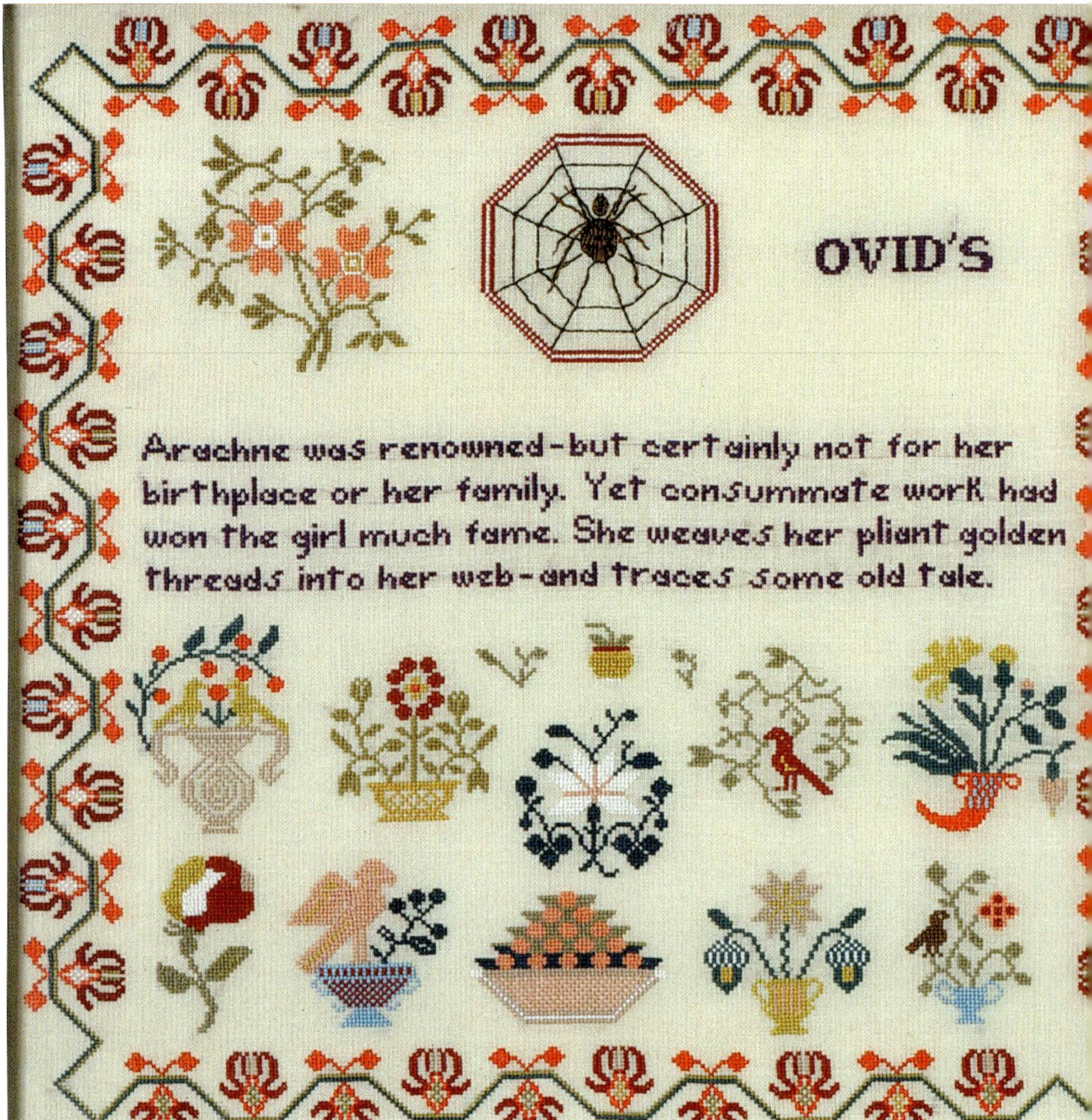

12. Elaine Reichek
Sampler (Ovid's Weavers)
1996

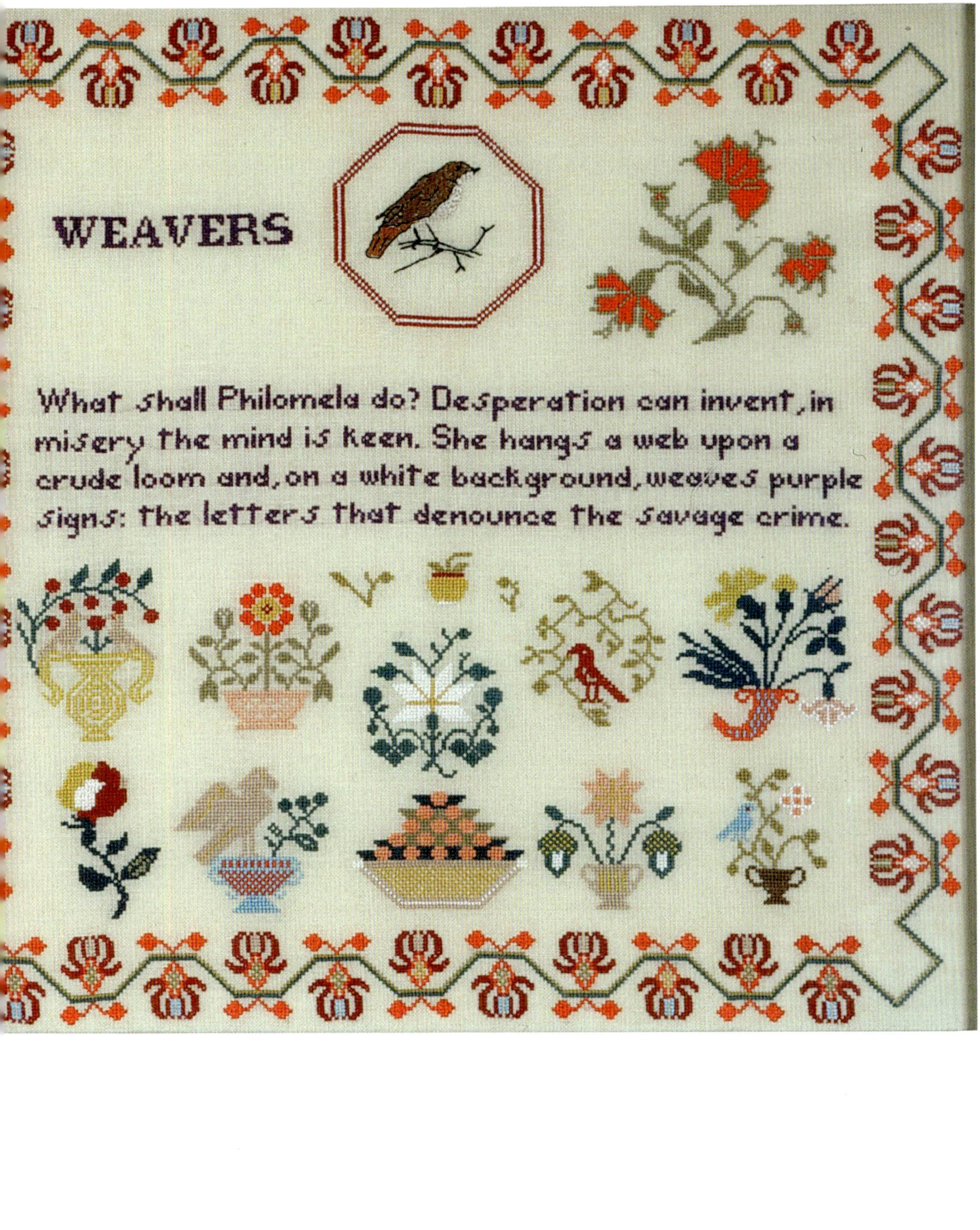
WEAVERS
What shall Philomela do? Desperation can invent, in misery the mind is keen. She hangs a web upon a crude loom and, on a white background, weaves purple signs: the letters that denounce the savage crime.

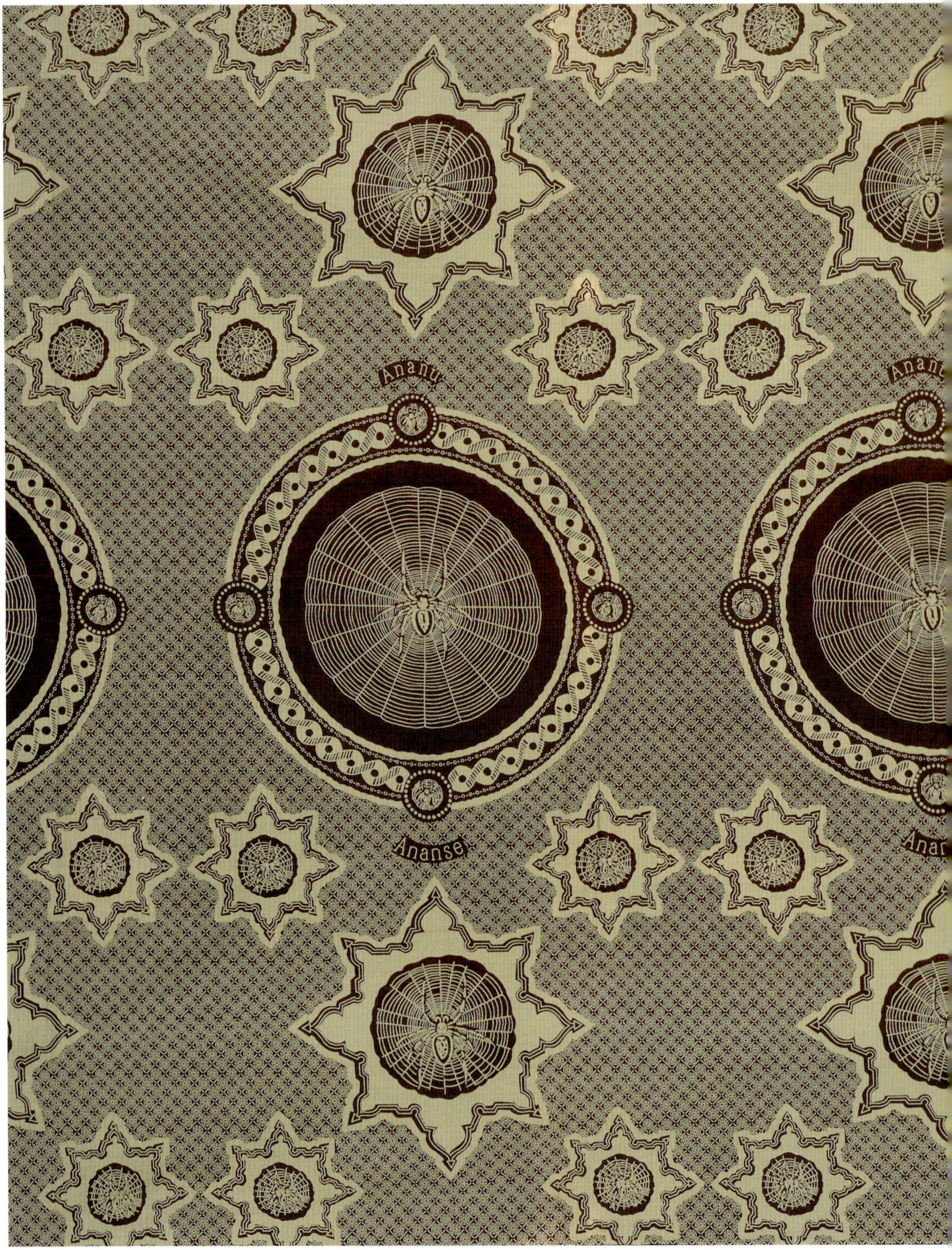
Ananu
Ananse

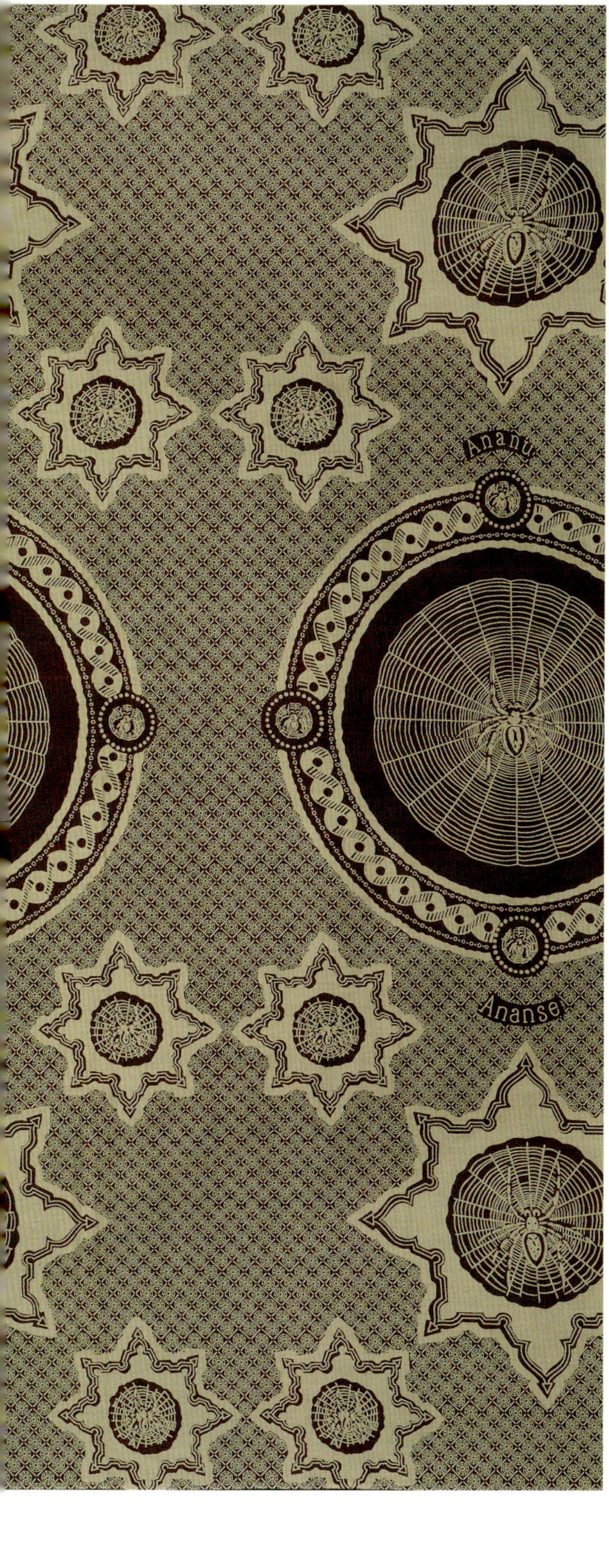

13. *Ananse Textile*
c. 1970

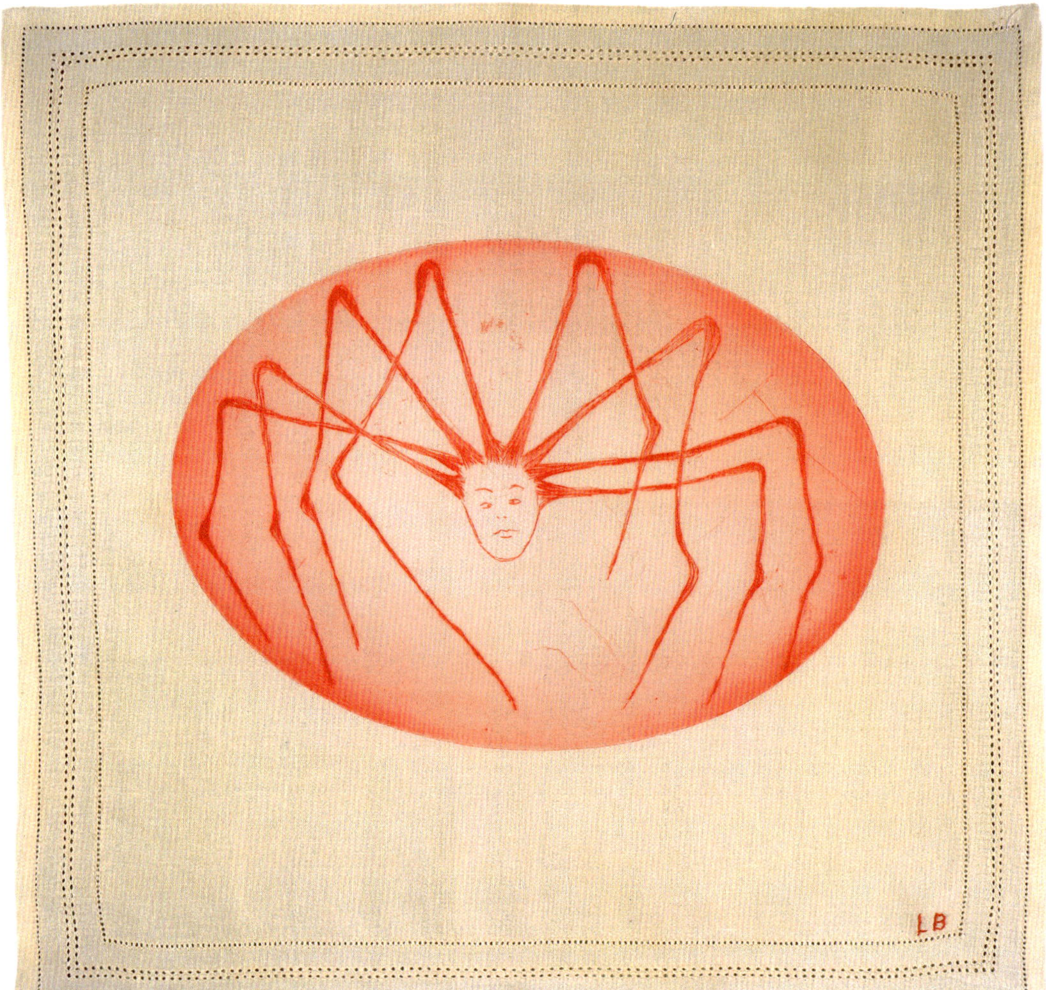
LB

14. Louise Bourgeois
Spider Woman
2004

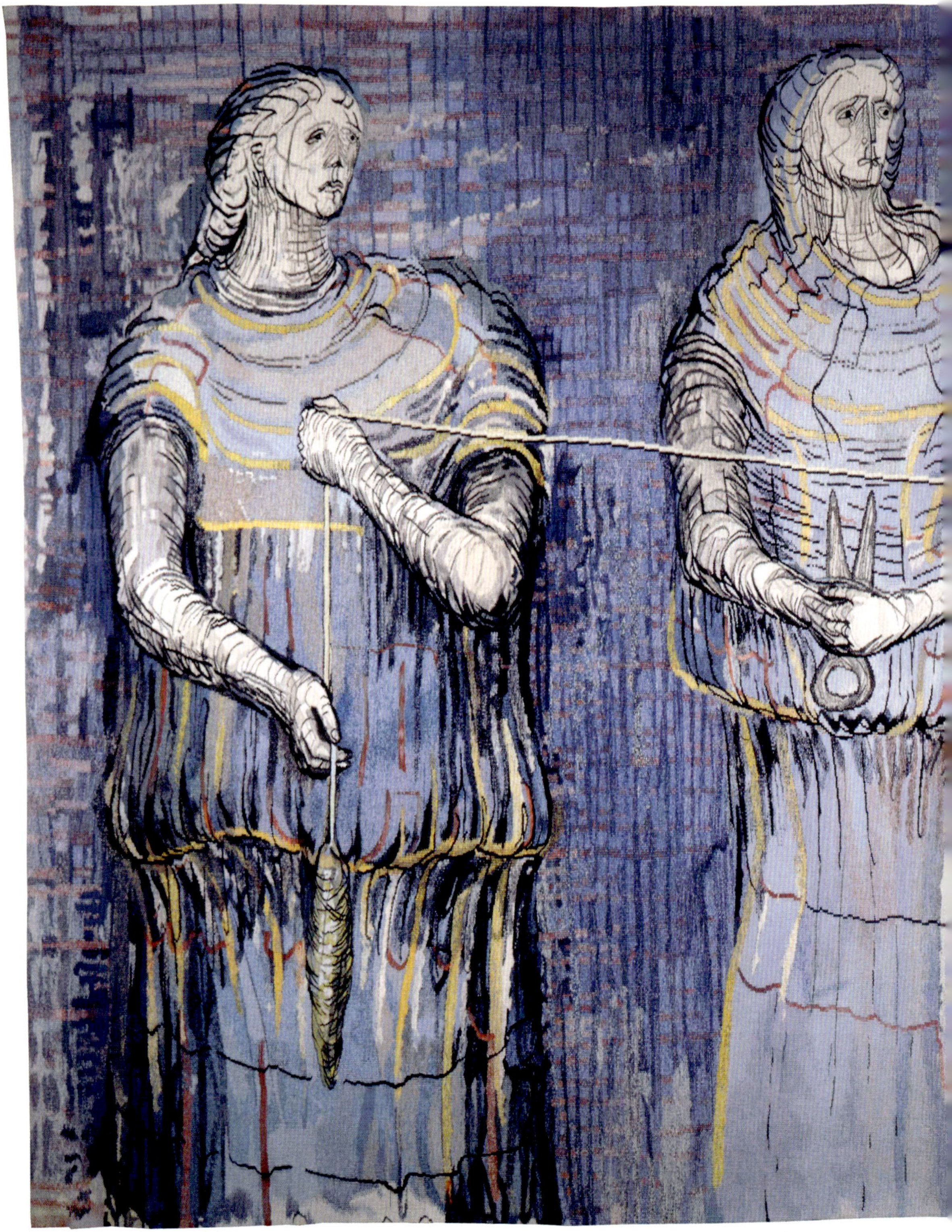

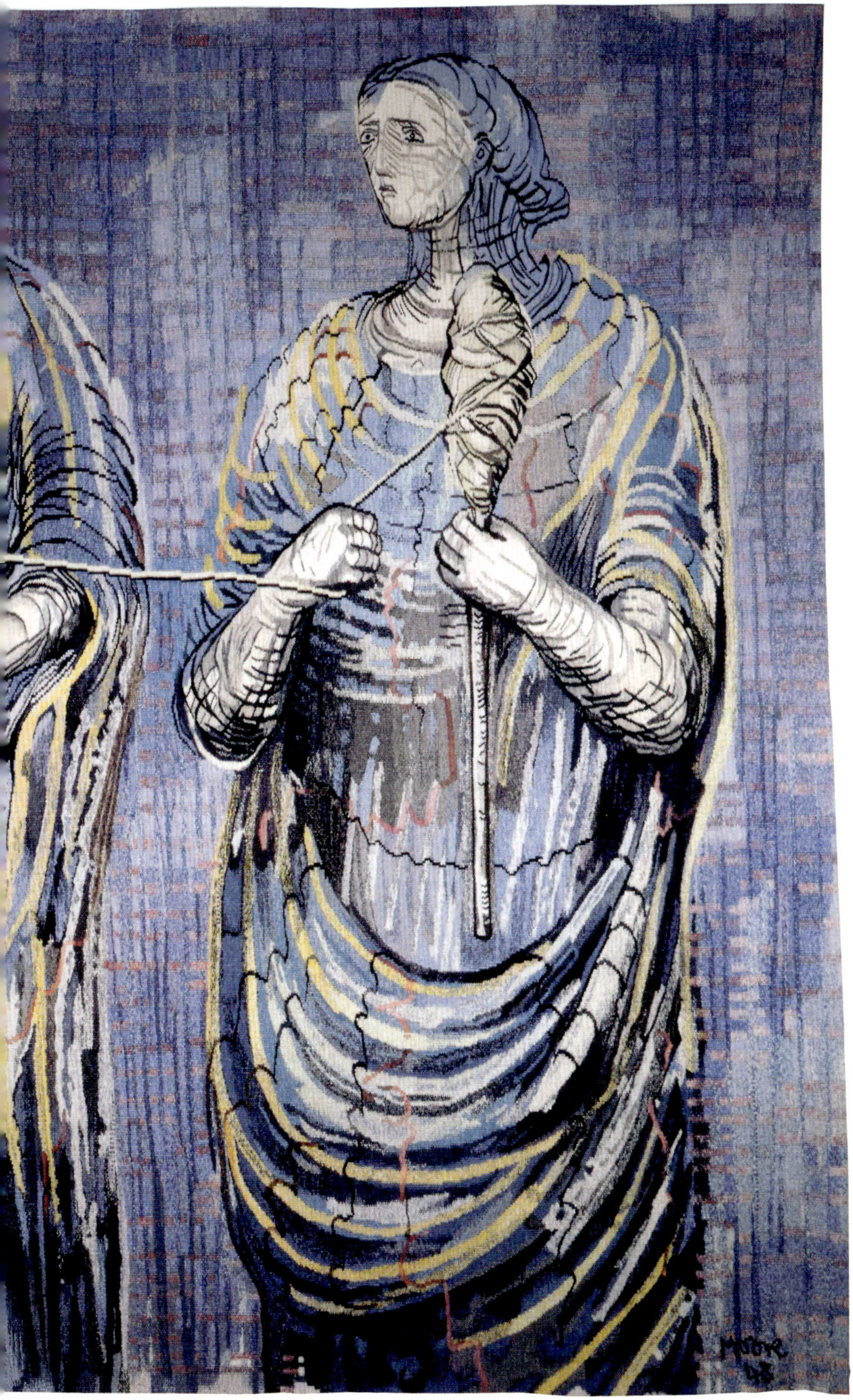

15. Henry Moore
Three Fates
1983–84

16. Edward Burne-Jones
Chaucer's 'Legend of Good Women' – Thisbe and Philomela
1864

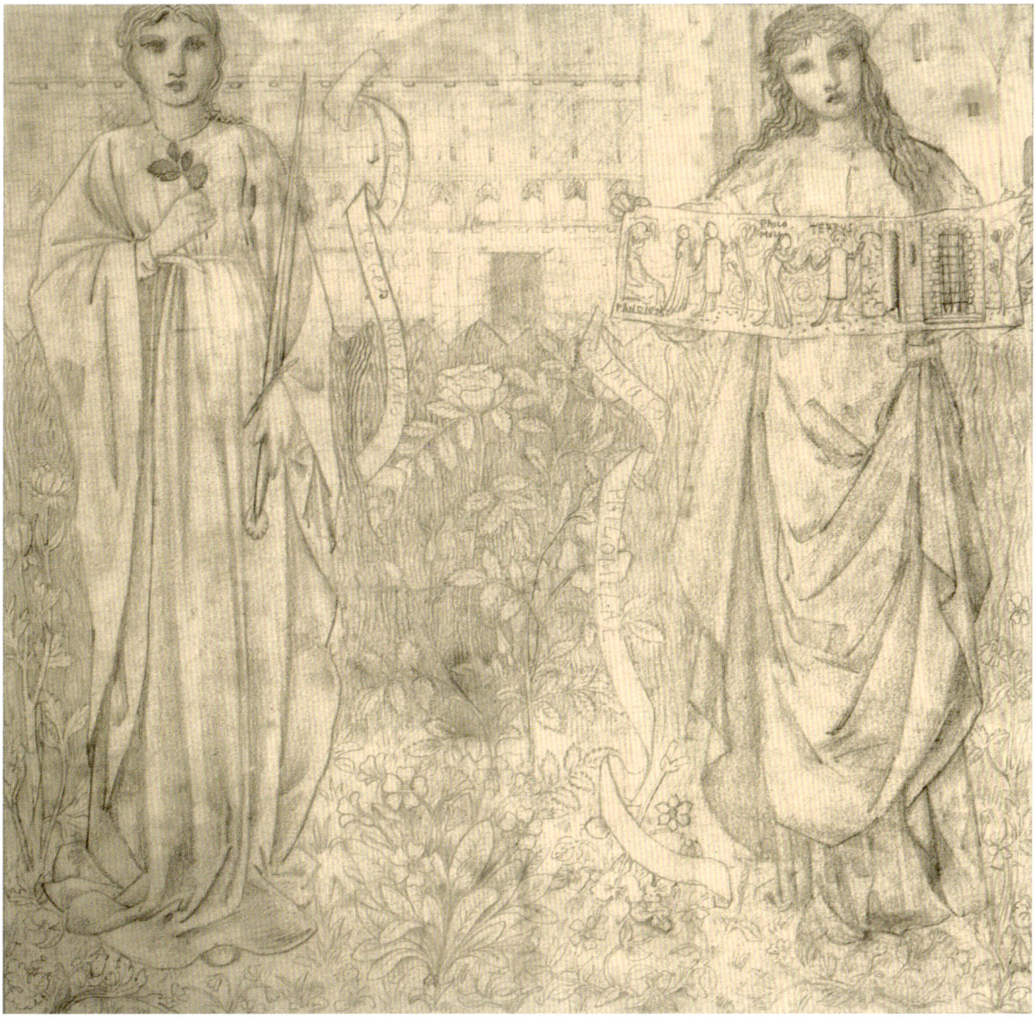
PANDION
TEREUS

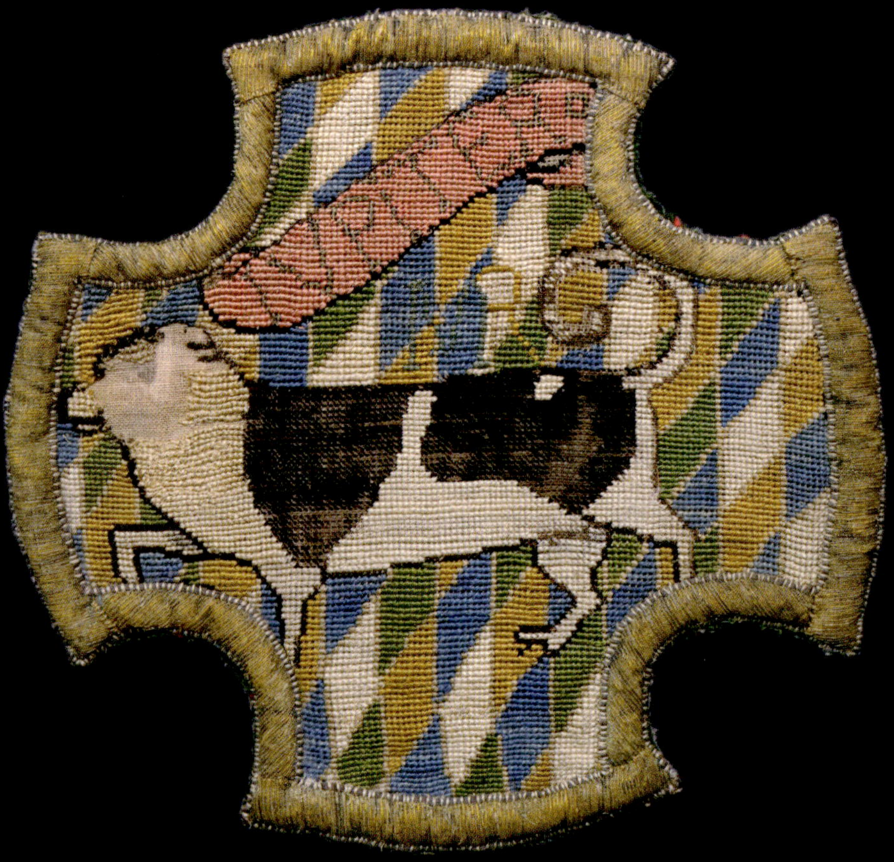

17. Mary Queen of Scots
The Oxburgh Hangings, Dog Motif
c. 1570

18. Ray Materson
The House on York Road
1994

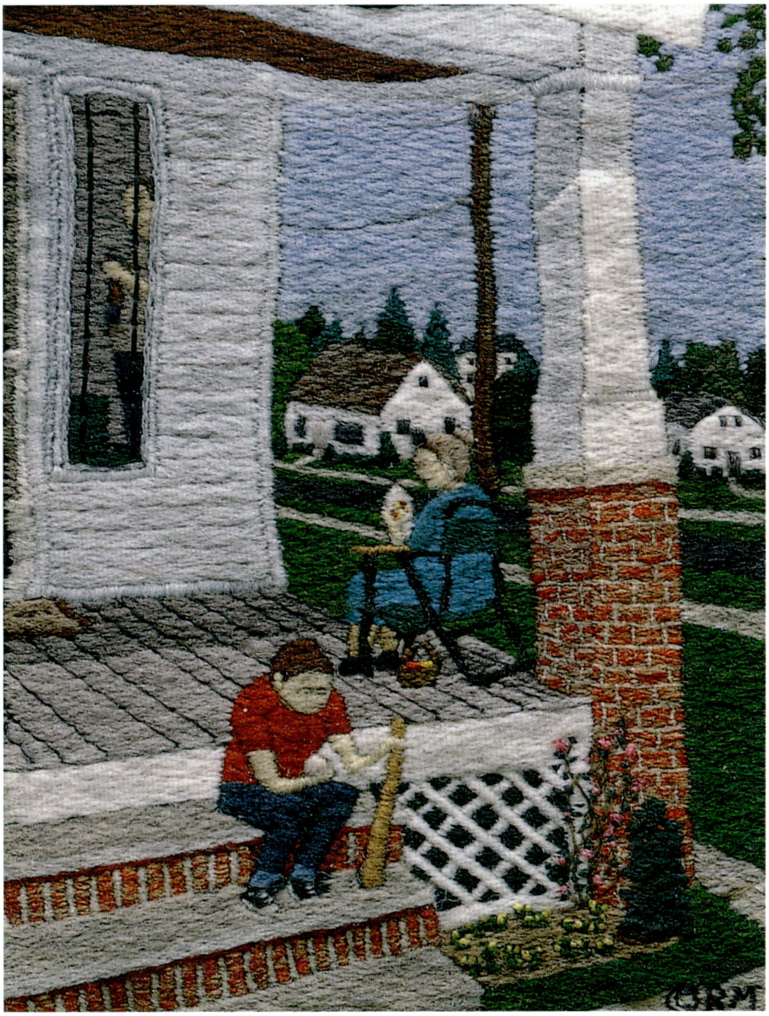
©RM

19. Ray Materson
First Cigarette
1992

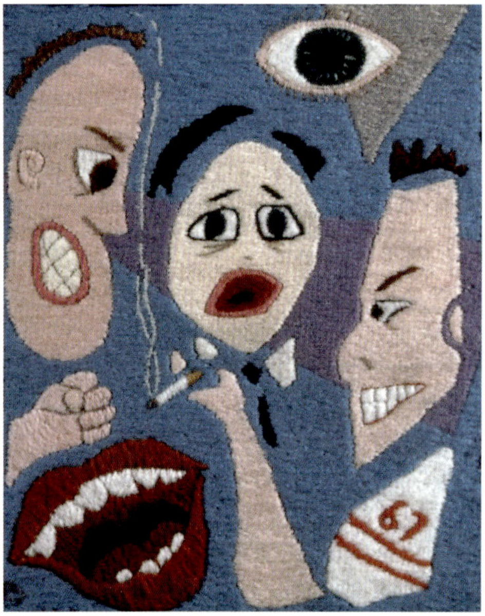

20. Ray Materson
Don't Get Pulled In
1992

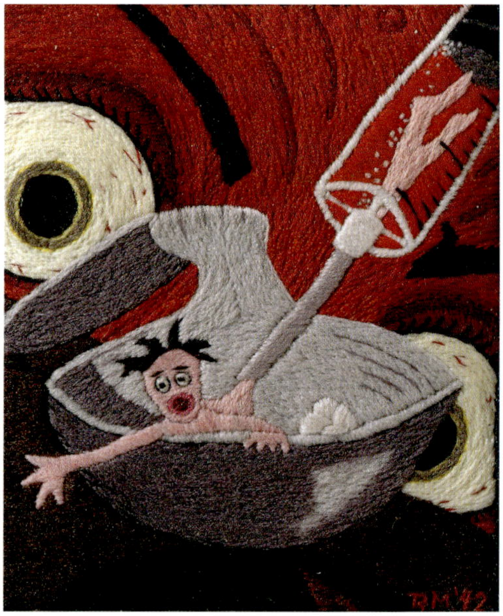

21. Ray Materson
Tiny: Life×6, The Noon Watch J2
1997

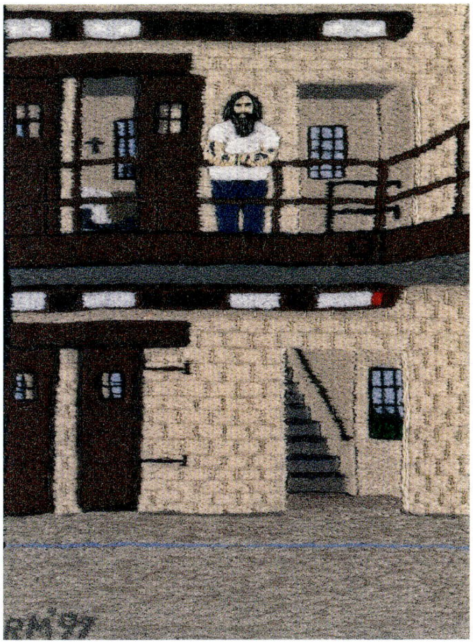

22. Ray Materson
The Trailer Visit
1994

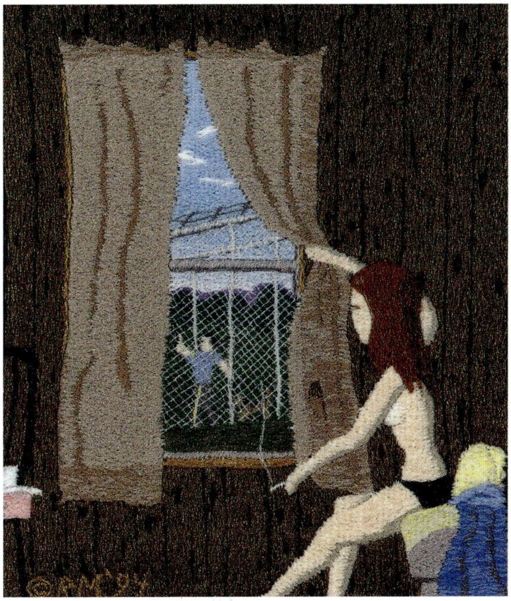

23. Ray Materson
Metamorphosis III
2007

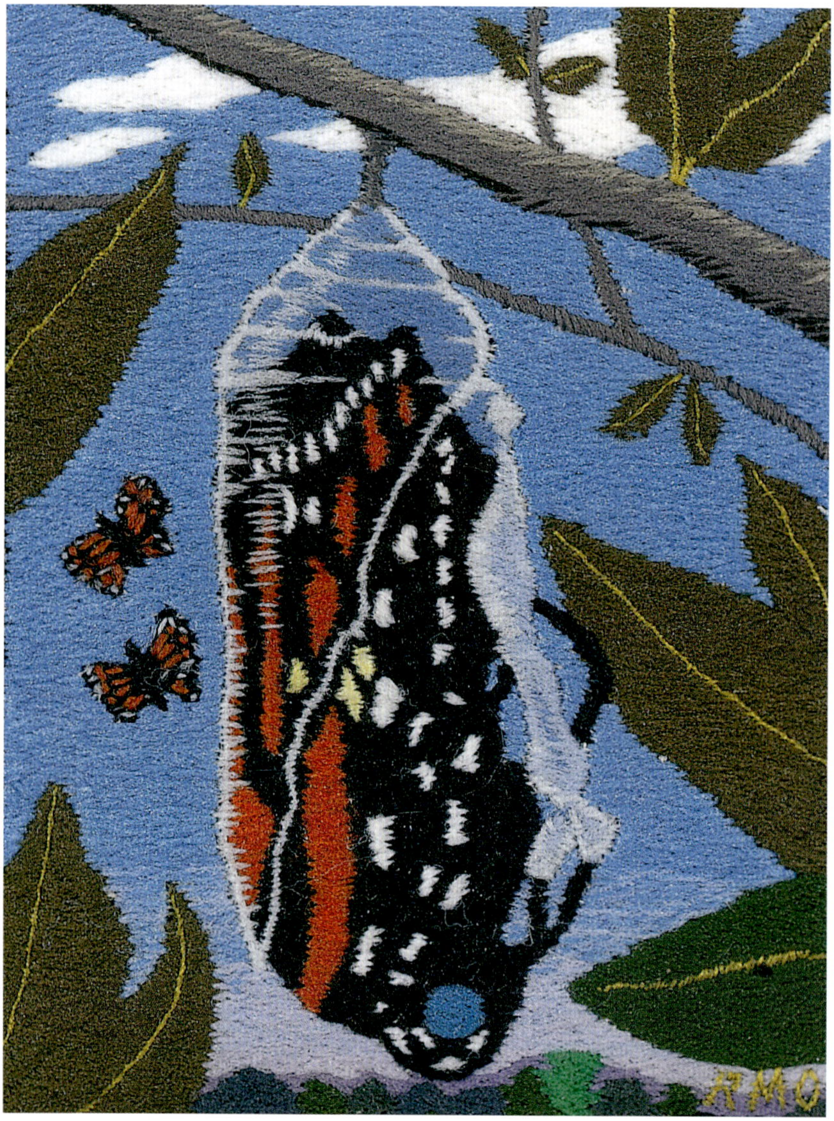

24. Judith Scott
Untitled
1990

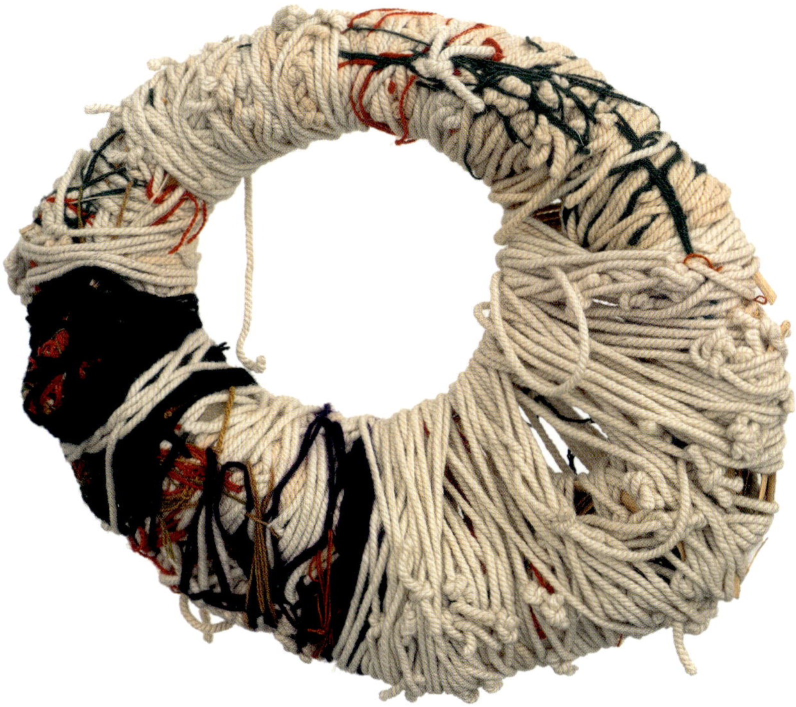

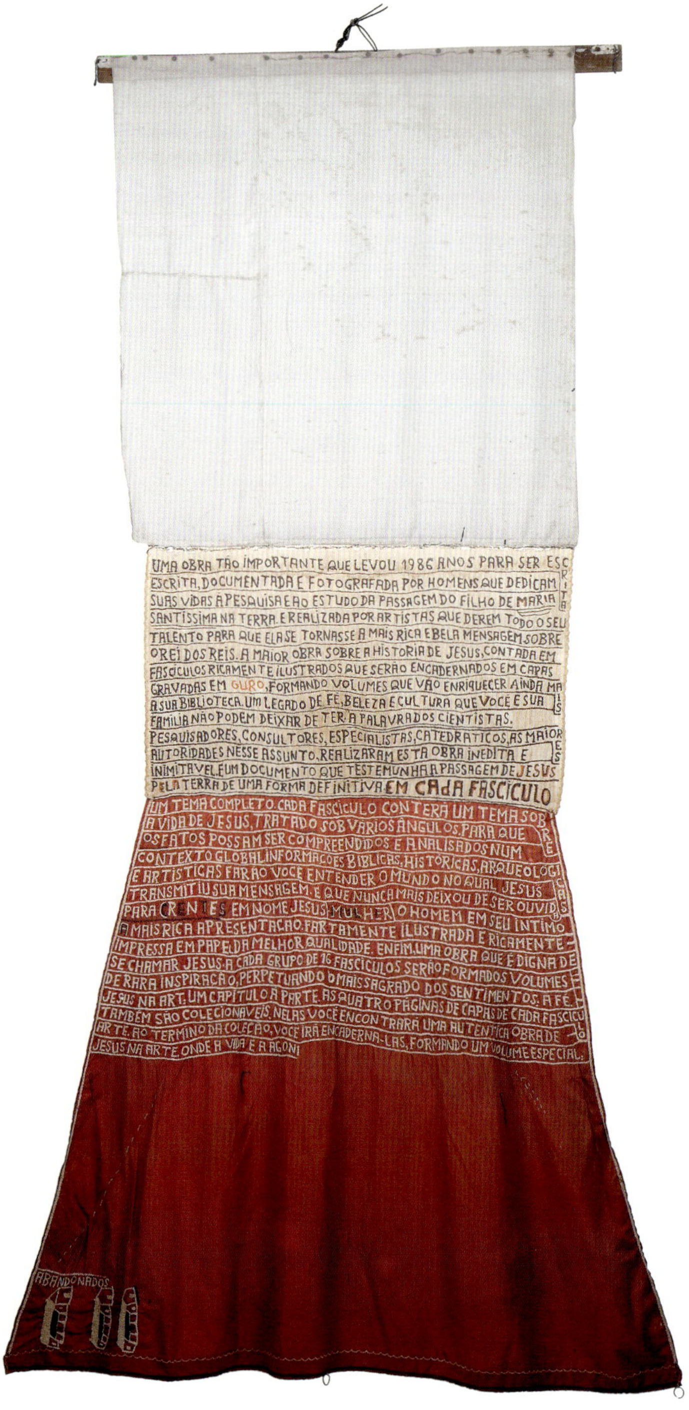
UMA OBRA TÃO IMPORTANTE QUE LEVOU 1986 ANOS PARA SER ESC
RITA
ESCRITA, DOCUMENTADA E FOTOGRAFADA POR HOMENS QUE DEDICAM
SUAS VIDAS A PESQUISA E AO ESTUDO DA PASSAGEM DO FILHO DE MARIA
SANTISSIMA NA TERRA. E REALIZADA POR ARTISTAS QUE DEREM TODO O SEU
TALENTO PARA QUE ELA SE TORNASSE A MAIS RICA E BELA MENSAGEM SOBRE
O REI DOS REIS. A MAIOR OBRA SOBRE A HISTORIA DE JESUS, CONTADA EM
FASCICULOS RICAMENTE ILUSTRADOS QUE SERÃO ENCADERNADOS EM CAPAS
GRAVADAS EM OURO, FORMANDO VOLUMES QUE VÃO ENRIQUECER AINDA MA
IS
A SUA BIBLIOTECA. UM LEGADO DE FÉ, BELEZA E CULTURA QUE VOCÊ E SUA
FAMILIA NÃO PODEM DEIXAR DE TER. A PALAVRA DOS CIENTISTAS.
PESQUISADORES, CONSULTORES, ESPECIALISTAS, CATEDRATICOS, AS MAIOR
ES
AUTORIDADES NESSE ASSUNTO, REALIZARAM ESTA OBRA INEDITA E
INIMITAVEL. É UM DOCUMENTO QUE TESTEMUNHA A PASSAGEM DE JESUS
PELA TERRA DE UMA FORMA DEFINITIVA EM CADA FASCICULO
UM TEMA COMPLETO. CADA FASCICULO CONTERÁ UM TEMA SOB
RE
A VIDA DE JESUS, TRATADO SOB VÁRIOS ÂNGULOS, PARA QUE
OS FATOS POSSAM SER COMPREENDIDOS E ANALISADOS NUM
CONTEXTO GLOBAL INFORMAÇÕES BIBLICAS, HISTÓRICAS, ARQUEOLOGI
CAS
E ARTISTICAS FARÃO VOCÊ ENTENDER O MUNDO NO QUAL JESUS
TRANSMITIU SUA MENSAGEM. E QUE NUNCA MAIS DEIXOU DE SER OUVID
A
PARA CRENTES EM NOME JESUS MULHER O HOMEM EM SEU INTIMO
A MAIS RICA APRESENTAÇÃO. FARTAMENTE ILUSTRADA E RICAMENTE
IMPRESSA EM PAPEL DA MELHOR QUALIDADE. ENFIM, UMA OBRA QUE É DIGNA DE
SE CHAMAR JESUS. A CADA GRUPO DE 16 FASCICULOS SERÃO FORMADOS VOLUMES
DE RARA INSPIRAÇÃO, PERPETUANDO O MAIS SAGRADO DOS SENTIMENTOS. A FÉ.
JESUS NA ART. UM CAPITULO À PARTE. AS QUATRO PÁGINAS DE CAPAS DE CADA FASCICU
LO
TAMBÉM SÃO COLECIONAVEIS. NELAS VOCÊ ENCONTRARÁ UMA AUTENTICA OBRA DE
ARTE. AO TERMINO DA COLEÇÃO, VOCÊ IRÁ ENCADERNA-LAS, FORMANDO UM VOLUME ESPECIAL.
JESUS NA ARTE. ONDE A VIDA E A AGONI
ABANDONADOS

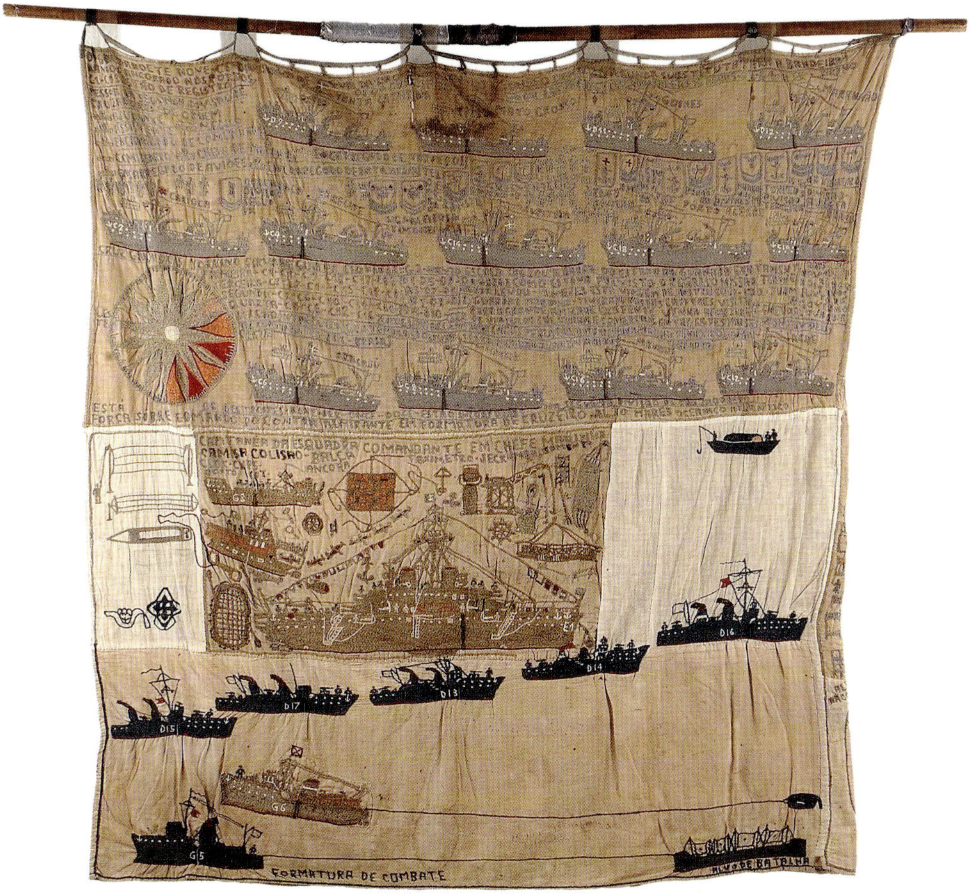

25. Arthur Bispo Do Rosário
Uma Obra Tão Importante Que Levou Anos Para Ser Escrita...(A Work So Important It Took Years to Write...)
1986

26. Arthur Bispo Do Rosário
Navios de Guerra (Battleships)
Date Unknown

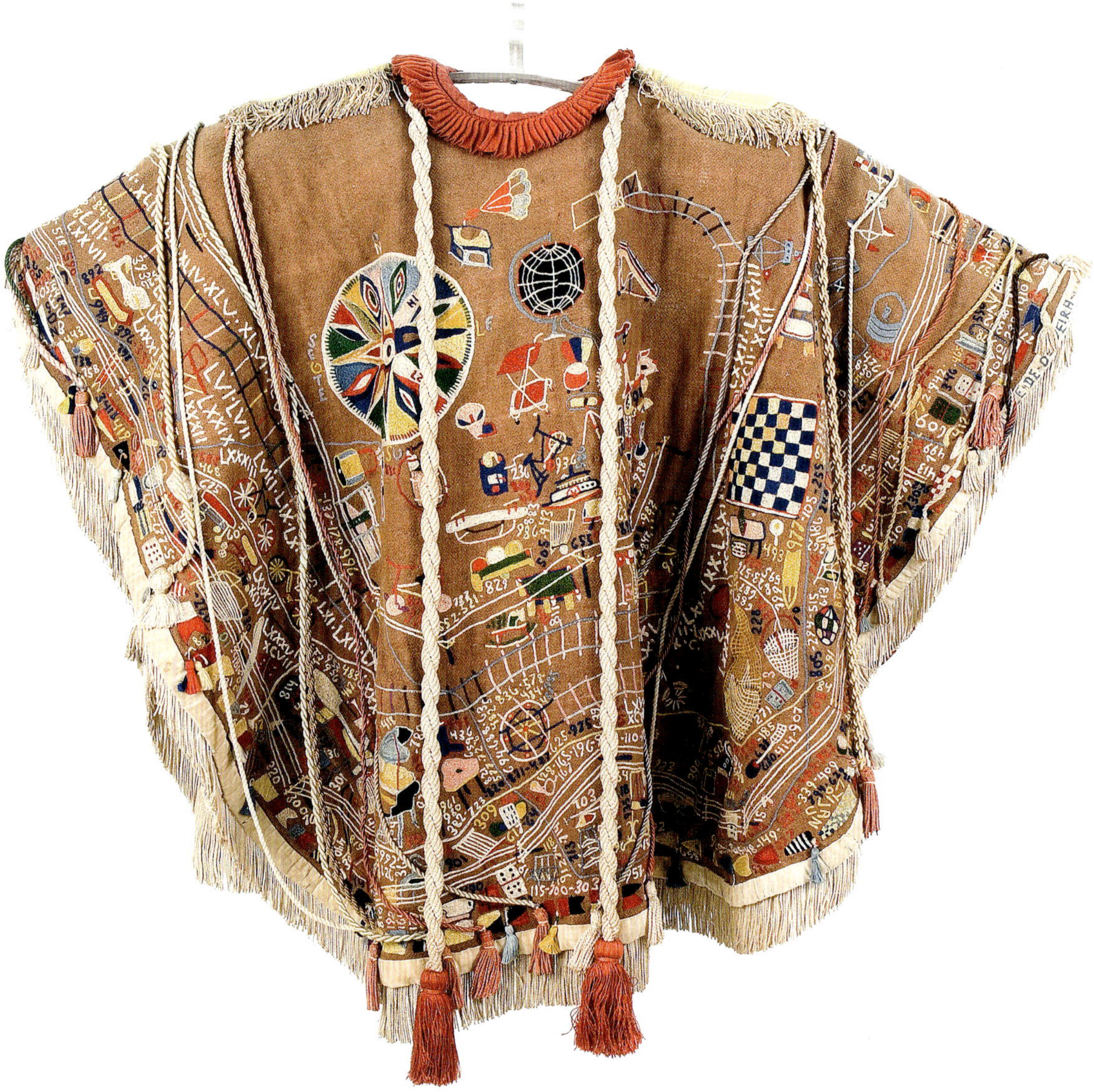

27. Arthur Bispo Do Rosário
Manto da Apresentação (Presentation Cape)
Date Unknown

28. Arthur Bispo Do Rosário
Cama de Romeu e Julieta (The Bed of Romeo and Juliet)
Date unknown

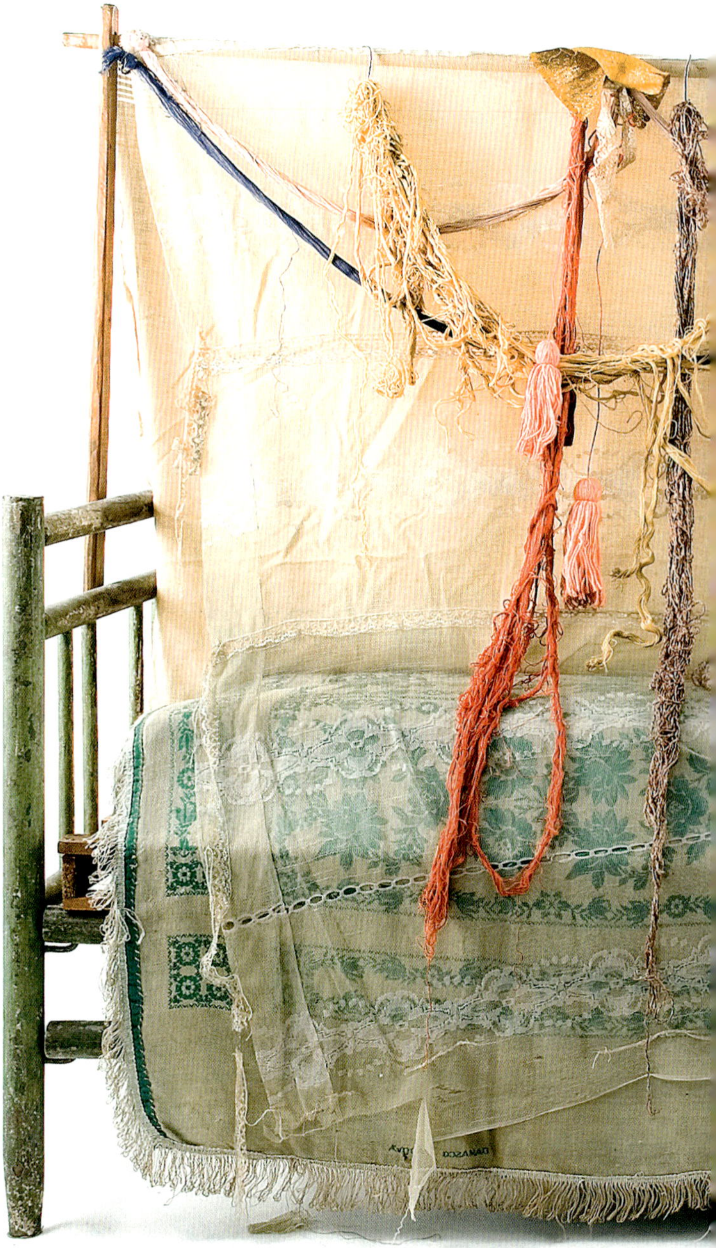

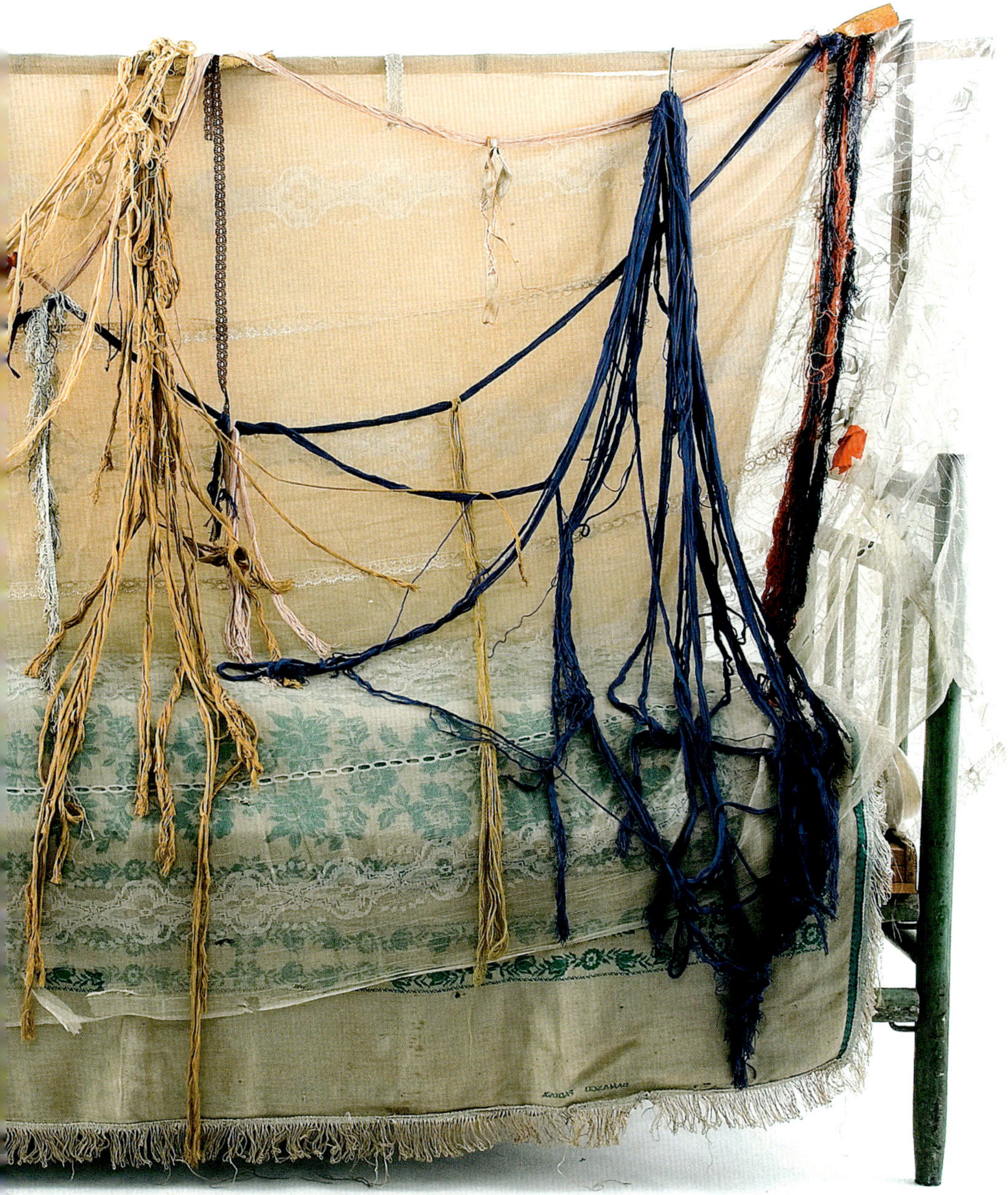

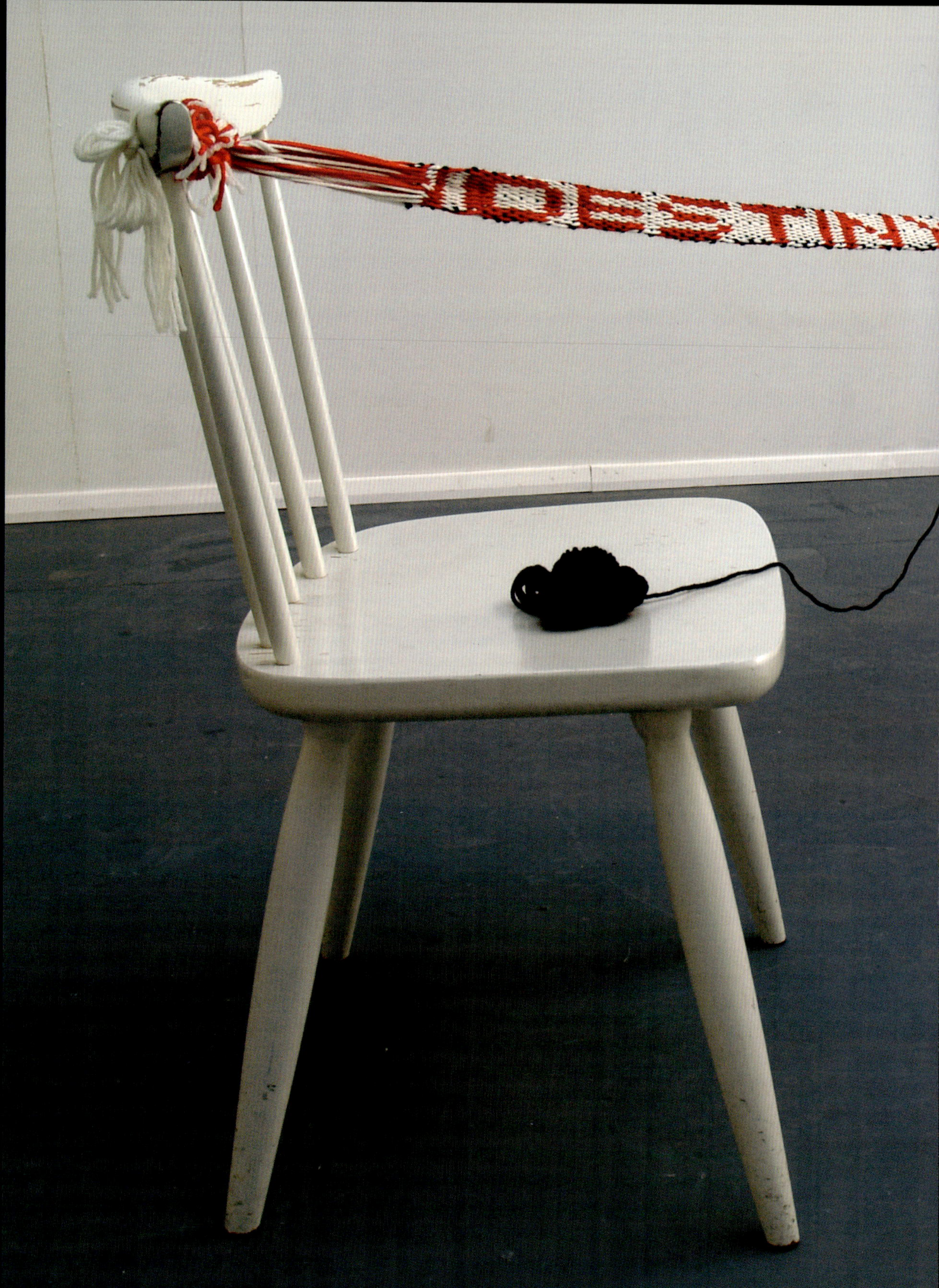
DESTI

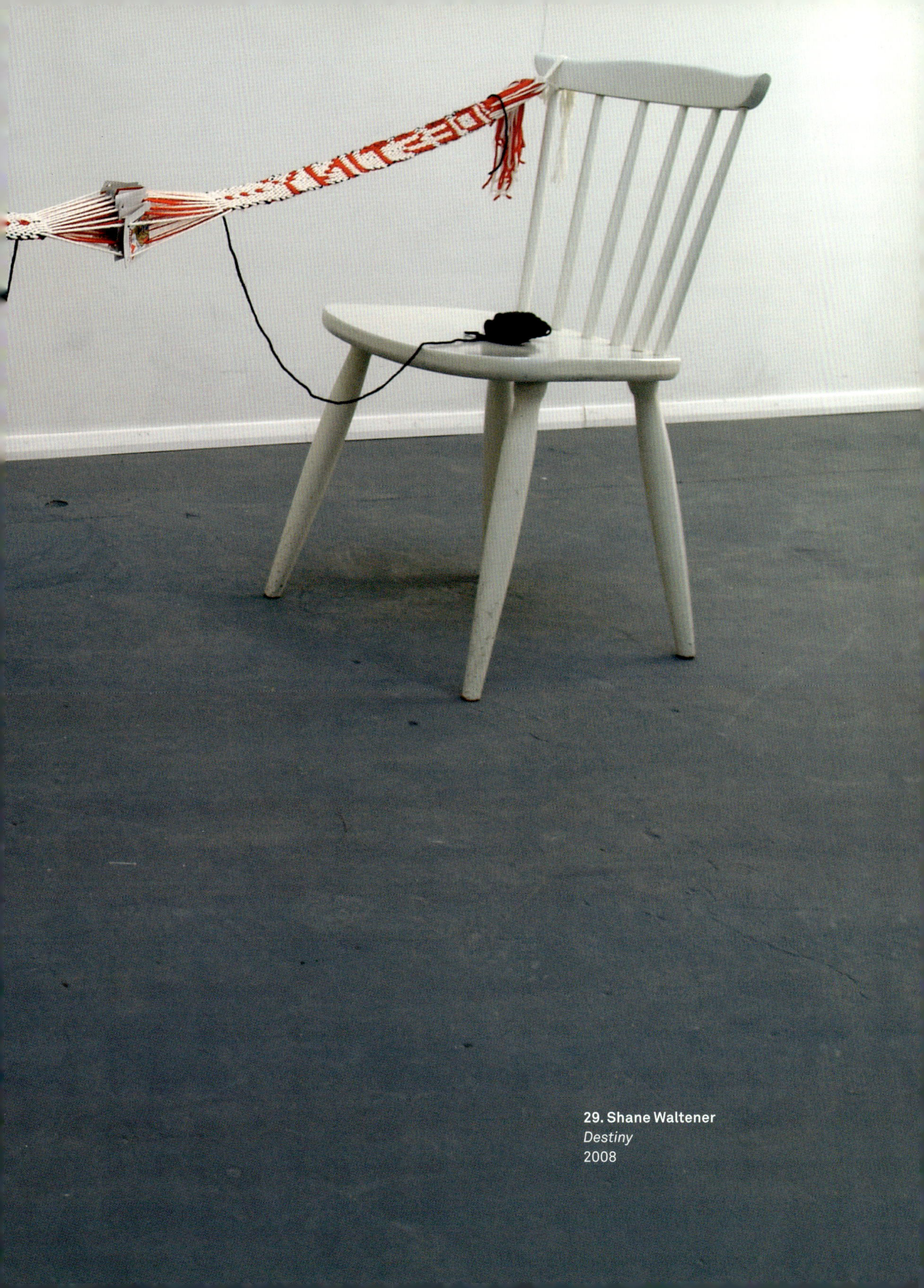

29. Shane Waltener
Destiny
2008

30. Artist unknown
Penelope
Date unknown

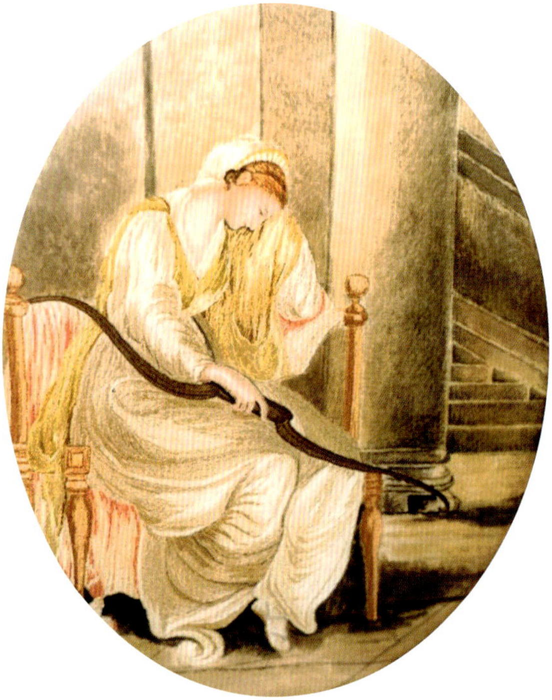

31. *Penelope Surprised by the Suitors*
1805

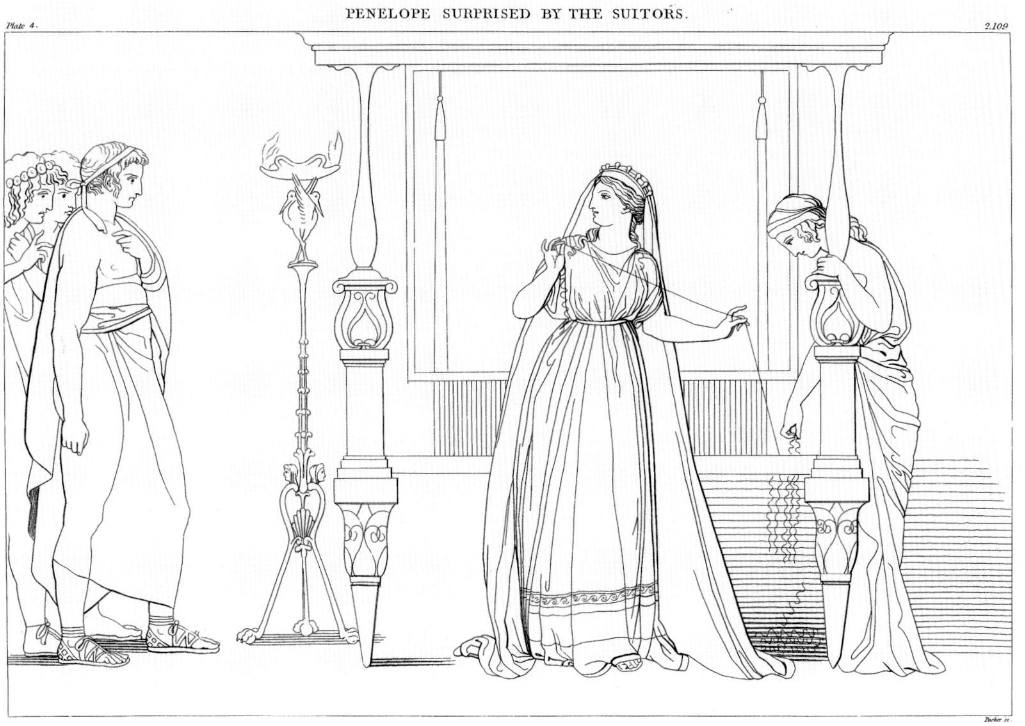

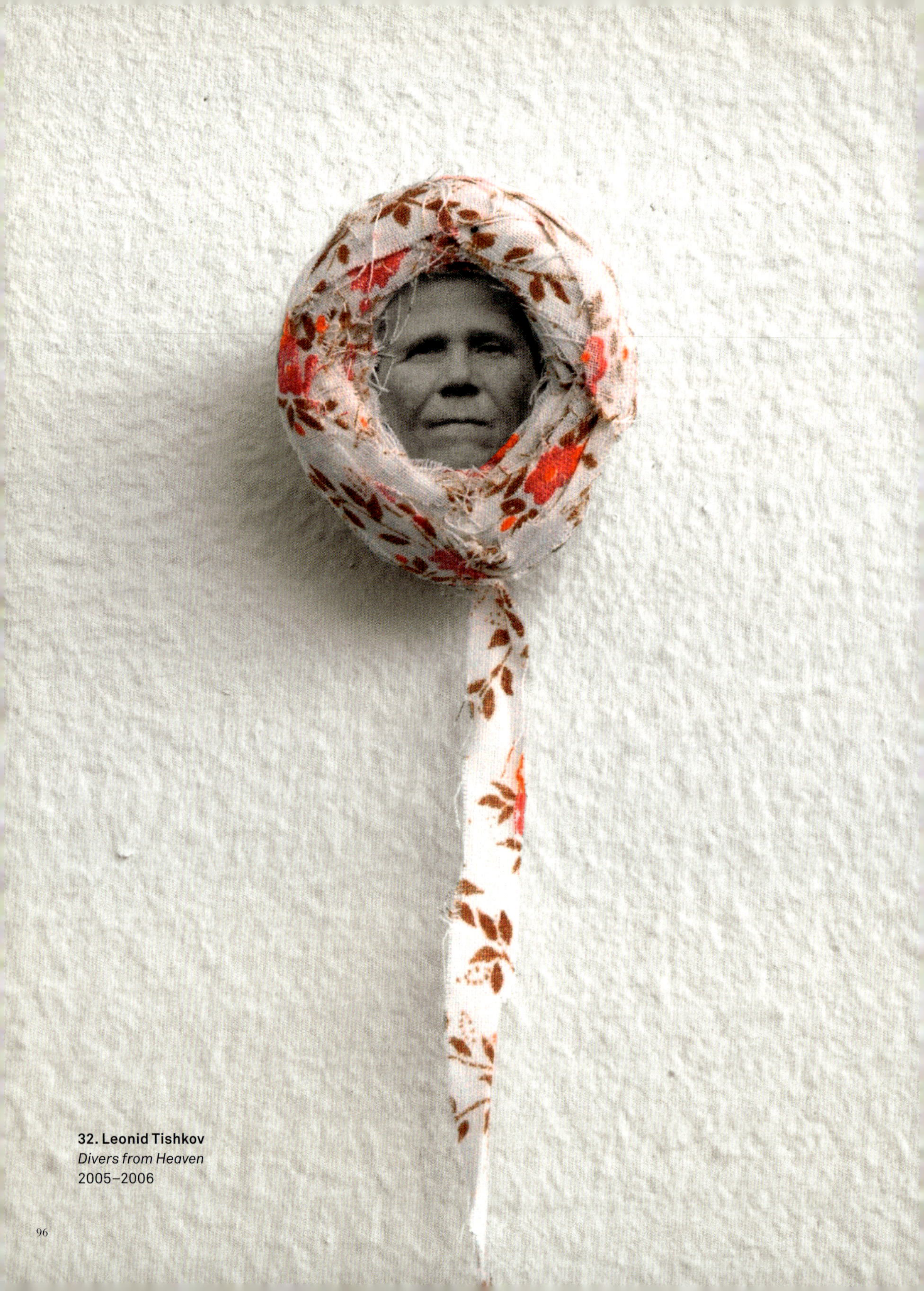

32. Leonid Tishkov
Divers from Heaven
2005–2006

33. Leonid Tishkov
The Vyazanik (The Knitling)
2002

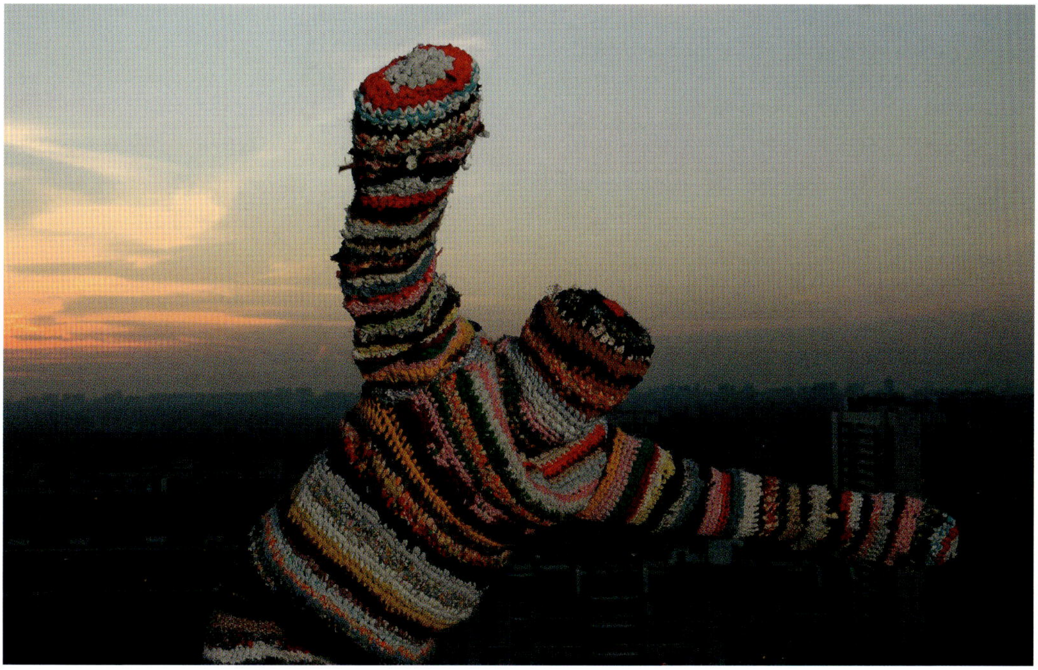

34. Delaine Le Bas
Gynaikonitides
2008

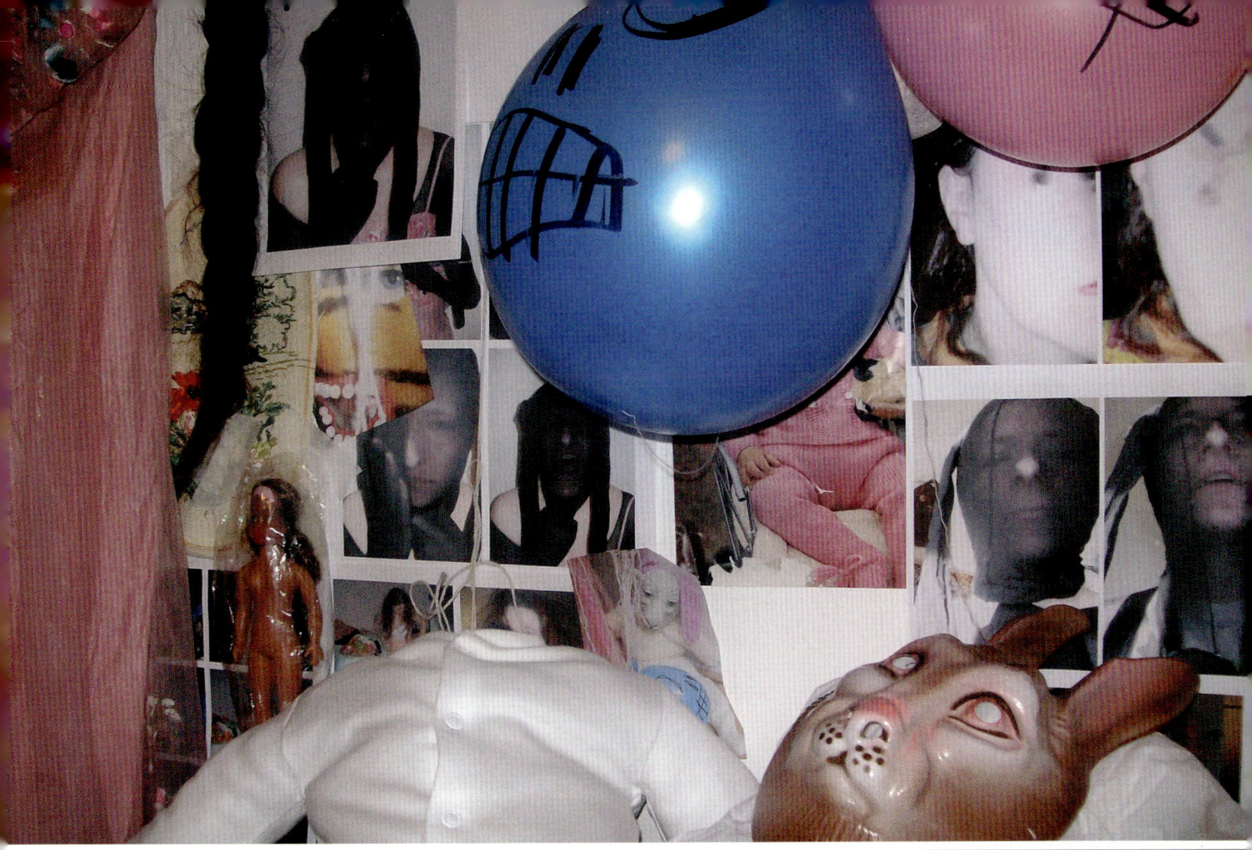

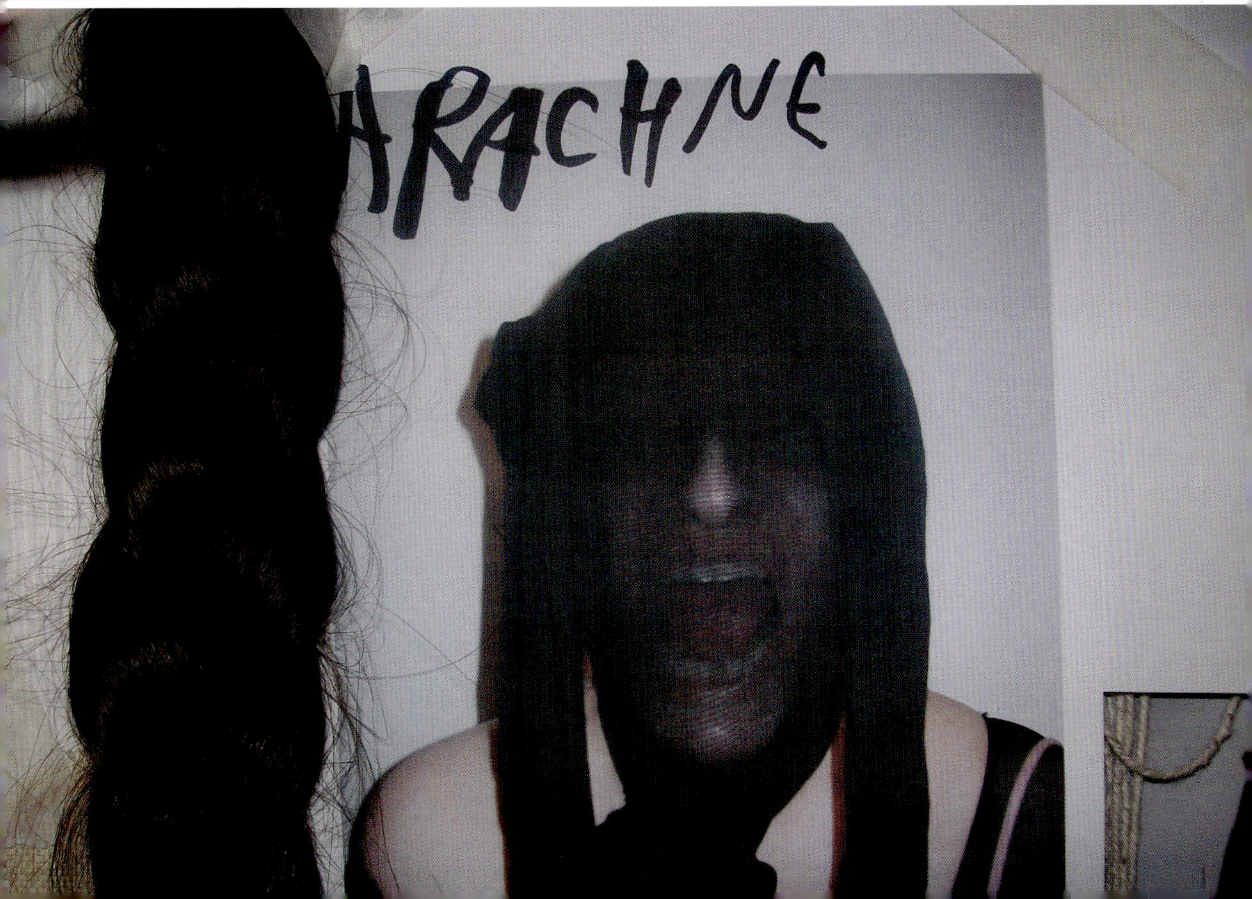
ARACHNE

35. Annie Whiles
The Moment Ago
2004

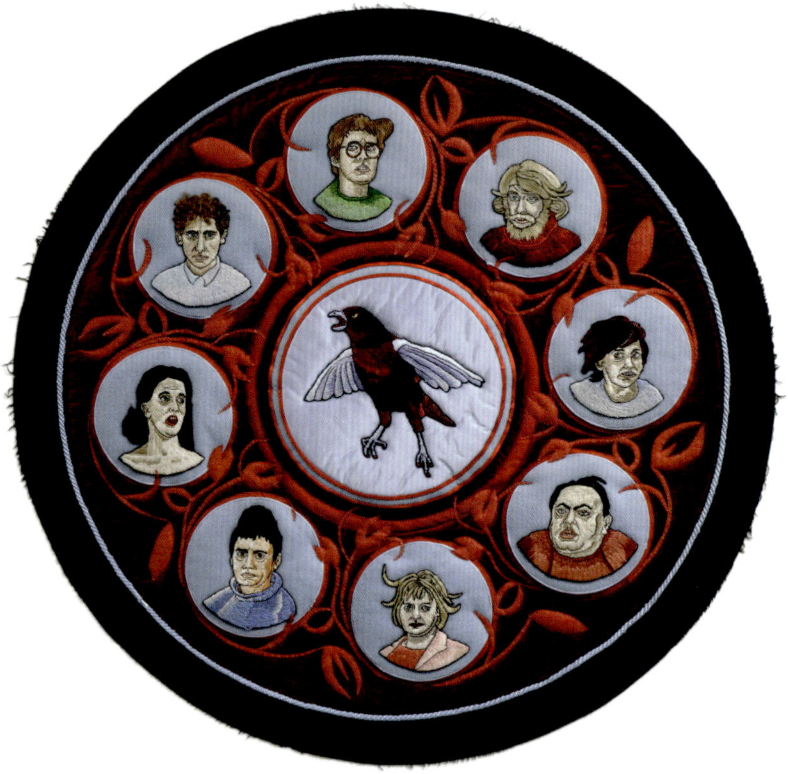

36. Michele Walker
Memoriam
2002

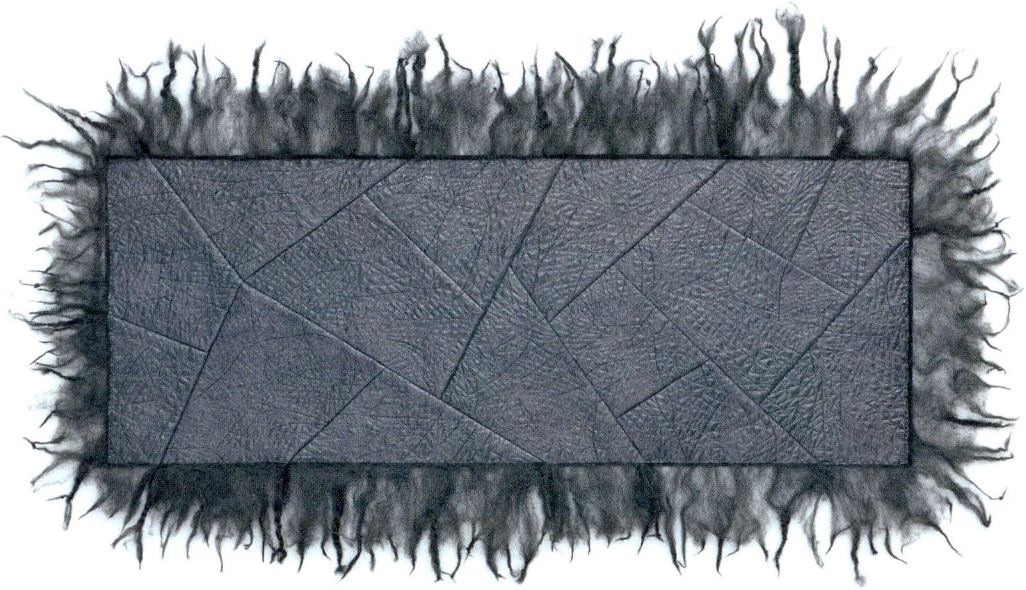

37. Tilleke Schwarz
Losing our Memory
1998

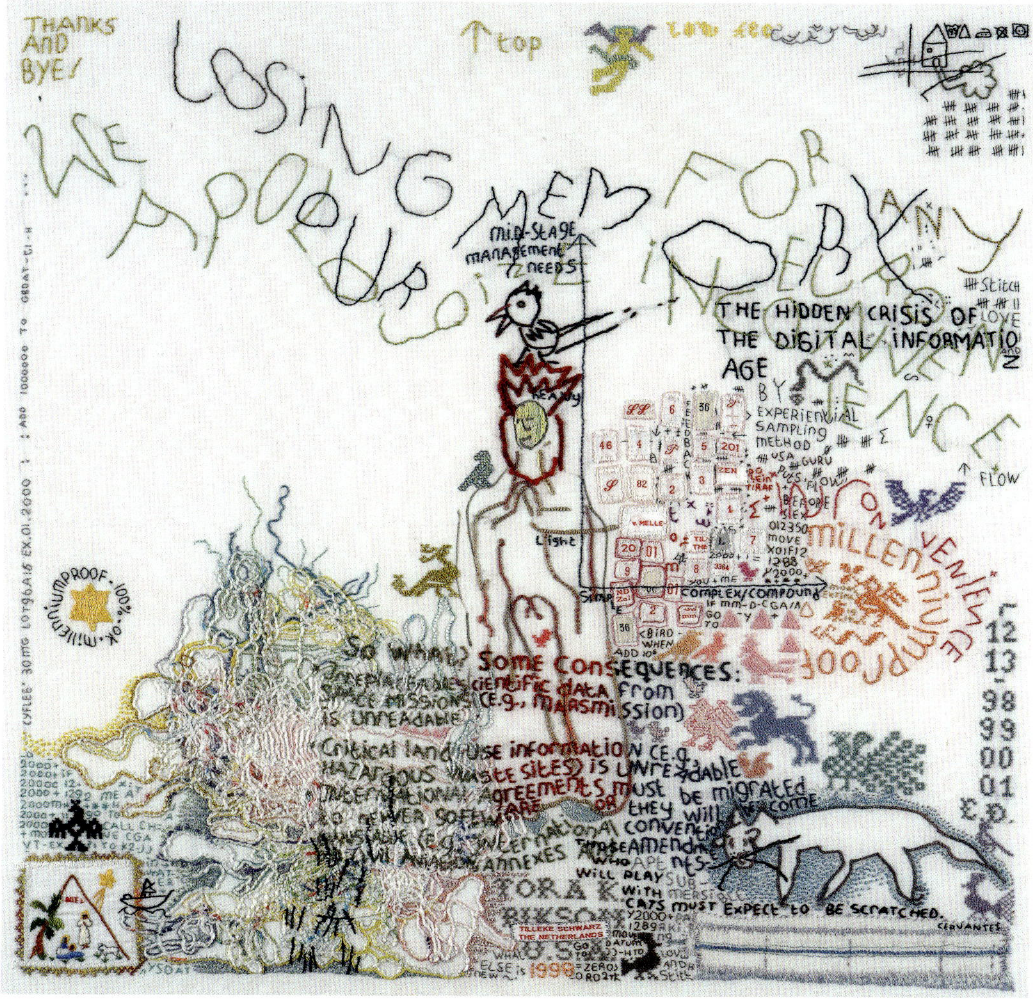

THANKS AND BYE!
↑top
LOSING
MEMORY
THE HIDDEN CRISIS OF THE DIGITAL INFORMATIO AGE
EXPERIENTIAL SAMPLING METHOD
COMPLEX/COMPOUND
So what? Some Consequences:
is unreadable
Critical land-use information (e.g. hazardous waste sites) is unreadable
international agreements must be migrated to newer software or they will become
WHO WILL PLAY WITH CATS MUST EXPECT TO BE SCRATCHED.
CERVANTES
TILLEKE SCHWARZ THE NETHERLANDS
1999
12 13 - 98 99 00 01

38. Joseph Beuys
Felt Suit
1970

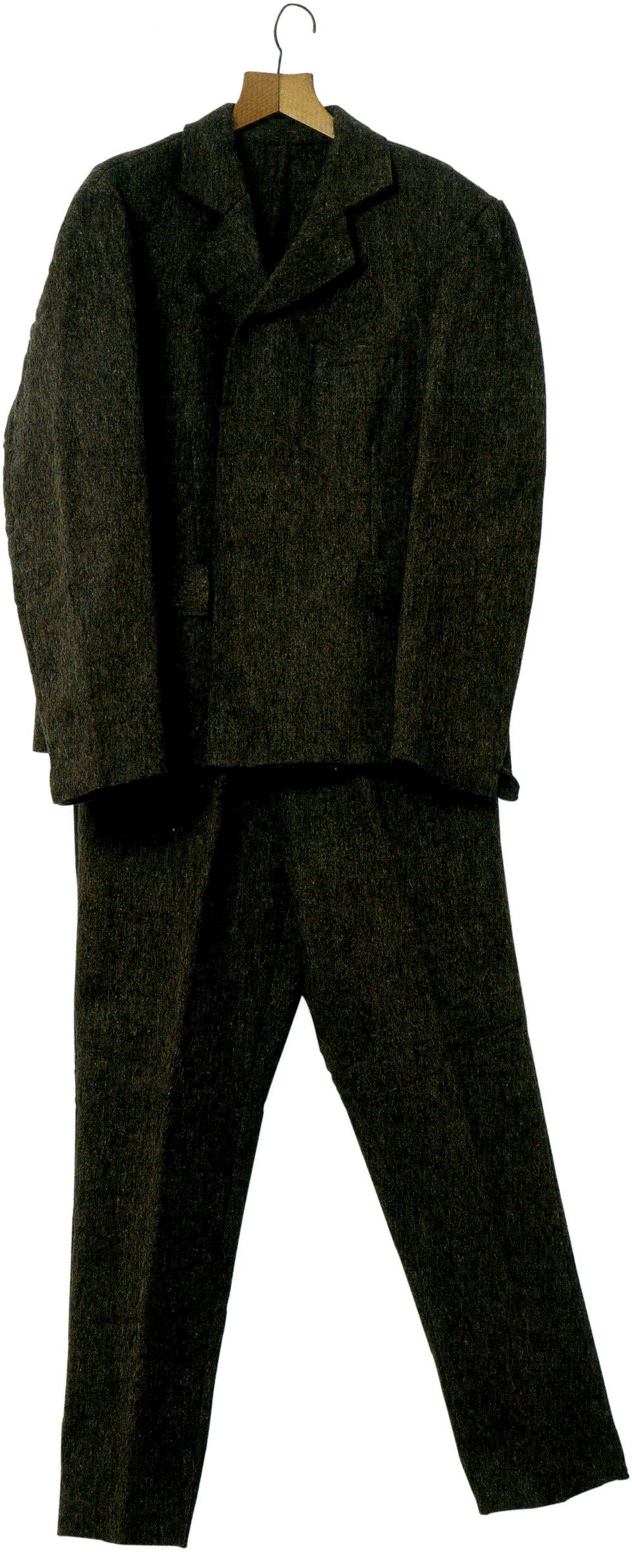

List of works

1
Ariadne and Theseus at the entrance to the Labyrinth
1563
From Ovid, *Metamorphoses* (ed J. Spreng), illustrated by Virgil Solis, Frankfurt am Main, Woodcut, based on an earlier woodcut by Bernard Salomon
16 × 11 × 2 cm
The Bodleian Library, University of Oxford
Douce O 36, fol.94r

2
Ariadne
5th century AD
Woollen tapestry
62.5 × 47 cm
Kunsthistorisches Museum Wien, Antikensammlung

3
Louise Bourgeois
Needle (Fuseau)
1992
Steel, flax, thread and wire
259 × 330.2 × 71.1 cm.
Galerie Karsten Greve, Cologne
Photo by Jochen Littkemann

4
Odysseus and Circe on the island of Aeaea
c1550–1600
Flemish Narrative Tapestry
275 × 232 cm
Jack & Linda Keenan, Intaglio Antiques, San Antonio, Texas
© Sotheby's

5
Odysseus and Circe
4th century BC
Boeotian (Cabirion) black figure skyphos (drinking vessel)
Height 15.4 cm
Ashmolean Museum, Oxford

6
William Morris
The Woodpecker
1885
Tapestry designed by William Morris and woven by Morris & Company
287.5 × 150 cm
William Morris Gallery, London

7
Europa and the Bull
1563
From Ovid, *Metamorphoses* (ed J. Spreng), illustrated by Virgil Solis, Frankfurt am Main, Woodcut, based on an earlier woodcut by Bernard Salomon
16 × 11 × 2 cm
The Bodleian Library, University of Oxford
Douce O 36, fol.36r

8
Elizabeth Hardwick, Countess of Shrewsbury
Europa and the Bull
c1580
Embroidered panel
58 × 132 × 7.7 cm
Hardwick Hall, the Devonshire Collection (acquired through the National Land Fund and transferred to The National Trust in 1959)
© NTPL/ John Hammond

9
William Holman Hunt
The Lady of Shalott
1857
Relief print on paper, engraved by J. Thompson
9.5 × 7.9 cm
Tate, presented by Harold Hartley, 1925

10
Alice Kettle
Metamorphosis
2003
Embroidery
67.5 × 67.5 × 1.2 cm
Private Collection

11
Arachne and Athena weaving contest
1497
From The Collected Works of Ovid
Illuminated manuscript
42.5 × 32.5 × 10.5 cm
Viscount Coke and the Trustees of the Holkham Estate

12
Elaine Reichek
Sampler (Ovid's Weavers)
1996
Embroidery on linen
56 × 95 × 4 cm
Collection of Melva Bucksbaum and Raymond Learsy
Courtesy Nicole Klagsbrun Gallery, New York

13
Ananse Textile
c1970
Batik textile
114 × 182 cm
The Whitworth Art Gallery, University of Manchester

14
Louise Bourgeois
Spider Woman
2004
Drypoint on cloth
39.4 × 39.6 cm
Collection of the Artist, courtesy Harlan & Weaver, New York
Courtesy Louise Bourgeois Studio

15
Henry Moore
Three Fates
1983–84
Tapestry woven by Pat Taylor and Fiona Abercrombie
Cotton warp, linen and wool weft
243 × 350 cm
The Henry Moore Foundation, acquired 1984
Reproduced by permission of the Henry Moore Foundation
Photo by Michael Muller

16
Edward Burne-Jones
Chaucer's 'Legend of Good Women' – Thisbe and Philomela
1864
Pencil on toned paper, laid down
Birmingham Museums & Art Gallery

17
Mary Queen of Scots
The Oxburgh Hangings, Dog Motif
c1570
Linen canvas embroidered with silk, edged with gold tissue
30 × 30 cm
Victoria and Albert Museum
Presented by the Art Fund

18
Ray Materson
The House on York Road
1994
Embroidery
13 × 9 cm
Collection of William Louis-Dreyfus, © Ray Materson

19
Ray Materson
First Cigarette
1992
Embroidery
13 × 9 cm
Collection of Sandi Blanda, © Ray Materson

20
Ray Materson
Don't Get Pulled In
1992
Embroidery
6.4 × 5.7 cm
Collection of Peter S. Brams, New York, © Ray Materson

21
Ray Materson
Tiny: Life × 6, The Noon Watch J2
1997
Embroidery
13 × 9 cm
Collection of William Louis-Dreyfus, © Ray Materson

22
Ray Materson
The Trailer Visit
1994
Embroidery
13 × 10 cm
Collection of William Louis-Dreyfus, © Ray Materson

23
Ray Materson
Metamorphosis III
2007
Embroidery
7 × 6 cm
Private collection, © Ray Materson

24
Judith Scott
Untitled
1990
Cane, bent wood, cotton rug yarn
51 × 41 × 13 cm
Collection Irish Museum of Modern Art, on loan from the Musgrave Kinley Outsider Art Collection

25
Arthur Bispo Do Rosário
Uma Obra Tão Importante Que Levou Anos Para Ser Escrita... (A Work So Important It Took Years to Write...)
1986
Wood, fabric, metal, thread and plastic
260 × 75 cm
Collection Museu Bispo Do Rosário Arte Contemporânea, Prefeitura da cidare do Rio de Janeiro, Brasil

26
Arthur Bispo Do Rosário
Navios de Guerra (Battleships)
Date Unknown
Wood, cloth, metal, thread and plastic
139 × 126 cm
Collection Museu Bispo Do Rosário Arte Contemporânea, Prefeitura da cidare do Rio de Janeiro, Brasil

27
Arthur Bispo Do Rosário
Manto da Apresentação (Presentation Cape)
Date Unknown
Fabric, thread, paper and metal
118.5 × 141.2 cm
Collection Museu Bispo Do Rosário Arte Contemporânea, Prefeitura da cidare do Rio de Janeiro, Brasil

28
Arthur Bispo Do Rosário
Cama de Romeu e Julieta (The Bed of Romeo and Juliet)
Date Unknown
Wood, fabric, metal, thread and foam
125 × 220 × 80 cm
Collection Museu Bispo Do Rosário Arte Contemporânea, Prefeitura da cidare do Rio de Janeiro, Brasil

29
Shane Waltener
Destiny
2008
Wool, playing cards, chairs
Courtesy of the Artist

30
Penelope
Date unknown
Embroidered picture of silk and thread
29 × 35 cm
Marx Lambert Collection, Compton Verney

31
Penelope Surprised by the Suitors
1805
From Homer, *The Odyssey*
Engraved from the compositions of John Flaxman
Illustrated manuscript
45 × 30 × 7 cm
Fellows of Brasenose College, Oxford

32
Leonid Tishkov
Divers from Heaven
2005–2006
Textile and photographs
Courtesy of the Artist

33
Leonid Tishkov
The Vyazanik (The Knitling)
2002
Textile
Courtesy of the Artist
Photo by Frank Herfort

34
Delaine le Bas
Gynaikonitides
2008
Mixed media
Courtesy Sonia Rosso and
Galerie Git Nourbakhsch

35
Annie Whiles
The Moment Ago
2004
Embroidery silks, canvas, velvet,
felt and hair
100 × 100 cm
Courtesy Danielle Arnaud
Contemporary Art

36
Michele Walker
Memoriam
2002
Textile, plastic, steel wire wool
250 × 140 cm
Courtesy of the Artist
Photo by Steve Gorton

37
Tilleke Schwarz
Losing our Memory
1998
Hand embroidery on linen
64.5 × 65.5 × 1 cm
Courtesy of the Artist
www.tillekeschwarz.com

38
Joseph Beuys
Felt Suit
1970
Felt sculpture
170 × 60 cm
Scottish National Gallery of
Modern Art, Purchased with
assistance from the National
Heritage Memorial Fund and
The Art Fund 2002

Fig. 9
Louise Bourgeois restoring a
tapestry fragment
1990
Photo by Peter Bellamy

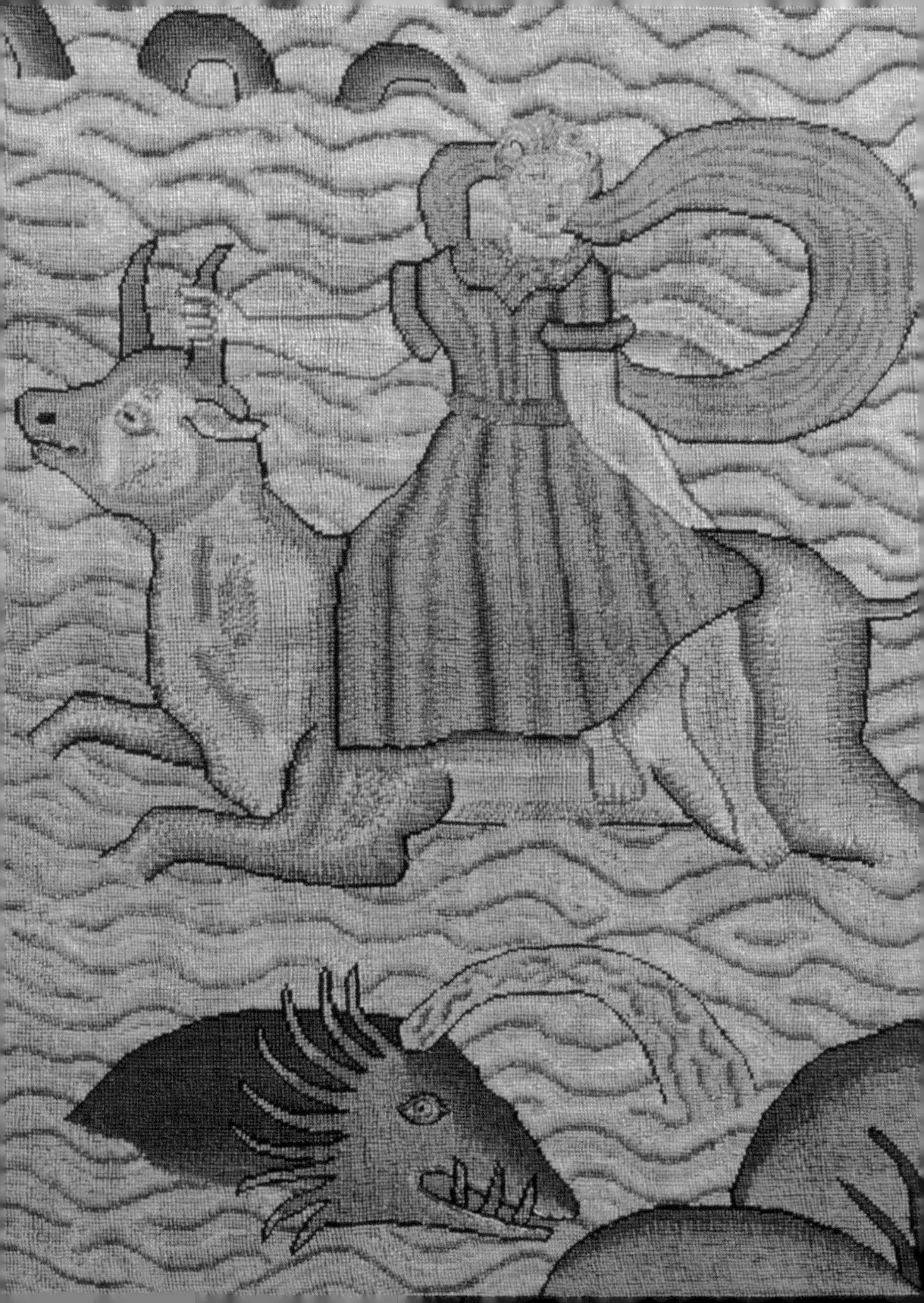